Suck
Squeeze
Bang
Blow

The Essential Manual
For The 21st Century Man

Hugh Slevin

To
CLARE
For
All The
Breakfasts, Dinners & Tease

Contents

Acknowledgements

I'd like to say a big thank you to Clive Dinsey for his help in developing and refining my skills and for acting as Technical Consultant on the project. Thanks Clive.

And another big thank you to Catherine at CBGraphics for her typesetting skills and patience.

Thanks also to Luke Trickett for the cover design & Watford Football Club for permission to use extracts from their Nicky Wright interview.

Suck, Squeeze, Bang, Blow

1

Maybe It Just Needs A Tune Up?

I believe in the Promised Land. And as you repeat that sentence again notice the changes that happen within you now as you hear yourself say I believe in the Promised Land. And as you speak those words again notice how your posture alters and your body begins to come alive as the images of all that is your Promised Land flow into your mind and how suddenly, as if by magic, now your world feels like a world of infinite possibilities. And as those images flow through your mind now make a mental note of what you see, is it something from the posters you had on your teenage wall when your dreams were of cars, motorbikes, guitars and girls or something to deal with the practicalities of today? Maybe adding a den to your castle so you can grab some me time, finding a way to put some extra cash in your pocket so you feel less stressed or loosing your love handles so you look good in your budgie smugglers as you strut your stuff on the beach. Or maybe it's a collage of both? But whatever it is for you, now you know three things for sure, it's all still out there, your dream is alive and well and you're right to believe in the Promised Land. Talk about reasons to be cheerful, well there's three.

OK, done that and I gotta say it works and feels good but my problem is still the same, how the hell do I make it happen in the real world? I'm ready to go and I've tried before but

just ended up feeling frustrated and pissed-off and doubting if I can really do it. It feels like I'm waiting for green and the lights are on endless amber. And trust me, feeling stuck ain't no fun when you know waiting won't make it happen.

Brilliant, now we're making real progress, you know what you want and you're prepared to put the work in to get it but your results so far have made you question your ability to get there. Well bravo to one and two and the third one is just a question of practicalities and by that I mean taking a fresh look at the methodology you've been using to get there. And if there's one thing us men are it's practical, just look at all the cool stuff in the world today and remember that we used to live in caves and run around in loin cloths chucking spears at wild beasts so the Missus would have something to cook for dinner. Now she just goes to the supermarket or easier still makes a few clicks on a mouse and the man from the supermarket delivers everything she wants right to your door. Talk about progress and that progress is a result of us men taking a practical approach and finding new and better ways to solve old problems and the good news is it works exactly the same way when it comes to you getting what you want.

OK, I'm still here and I'm still listening.

Good stuff, you feel free to space yourself out for a spell and as you get comfortable I'll continue. We're all men here, we stand up to take a leak and faced with a problem we want a practical solution that delivers tangible results fast, because then we can sit back and admire our achievements. And because we want results we're willing to learn new skills and do the work to get the job done so the fact we're all boys together is the ideal place to start from.

Our problems start when we're trying to do something and it's just not coming together like we want. Think of it like this, you've got some flat pack furniture to assemble so you grab your tools and get to it but the job's not going as smoothly as you hoped so after some tinkering and swearing you decide to consult the instructions wherein you find there has been a design change since you last did the job. And this change means the assembly method has also changed but now fully clued up you're soon in tune with the new how to and so you get the job done without further delay. Hands up who's been there? Well it works exactly the same when a man is working on getting to his Promised Land, if he is barking up the wrong tree the result will always be frustration, leaving him feeling pissed-off and doubting his abilities. The smart move of course is to put on your practical head and take a fresh look at the methodology you've been using and the good news is that's what we're going to be doing, getting a tune-up from the neck up so you can find a new way to solve an old problem.

OK, still here, sounds like it's worth hearing so I'm definitely listening.

Terrific, now before we move on let's explode a myth once and for all so you can move on and leave all the nonsense behind you now and forever. It's been suggested there are rules based on circumstance, either personal or physical, that govern a man's ability to reach his Promised Land and if these are not in his favour he'll be left facing a lifetime of frustration spinning his wheels stuck on the wrong road.

Point out that guys of every shape, size, age, colour and creed, with and without a high level of education, have successfully steered their way through to their Promised Land and the claim is they are just the exception that proves the rule. Look around you and see the number of your fellow men who qualify as the exception to the rule and the only logical conclusion you can draw is that the rule was maybe true once but is no longer valid, just look at the guys who have landed on these shores as penniless refugees but are now doing very nicely. Travel anywhere on the planet and ask a successful guy what they consider the most important factors in their success and the common answer is that they kept their eyes fixed on where they were headed and did enough of the right things to get there. And what does that tell us? Two things, firstly, the laws of success are universal and secondly, if you follow them they will work for you too.

OK, I see your point, you mean no excuses. I guess you can have a life of excuses or the life you really want but you can't have both.

Exactly. Although excuses do illustrate that you do always have choices in life. Some choose to excuse themselves out of living life in their Promised Land and that's fine, so long as it was a conscious decision and they are willing to live with the consequences of it. But that wasn't what you chose for you, you rejected the could have, would have, should have route and decided to chose the smart option and follow a different route so you cut out the middle-man of excuses, took responsibility and chose to direct your efforts at getting to your Promised Land.

2

What Do You Know About Motors?

So, what do you know about motors?

What's to know? I just turn the key, slide the gearstick into D, put my foot on the go pedal and slip into my driving reverie.

And it's just the same for millions, if not billions, of other guys. Talk about the practical man, when you think about it it's amazing what we can train ourselves to do automatically. It's like we have an internal autopilot that we trust to get the job done without us having to stop and think about how to do it. Anyway, we were talking about motors so check this phrase out and tell me what it conjurors up in your mind. Suck, Squeeze, Bang, Blow.

It would be easy to let my imagination run wild at that but if I remember rightly that's how an engine works.

Spot on, the fuel and air mix is sucked into the cylinder where it gets   squeezed by the piston, the spark plug ignites it to give you the bang and the blow is when the burnt gasses are ejected from the exhaust. Next up is ECU, so what pops in your head as you read that?

Er, engine control unit, the chip that tells the car what to do.

Spot on again, it's the electronic brain that was designed to keep your engine running at its optimum level. And on the chip is a software programme that was specifically written for the make and model you drive and its job is to ensure your engine goes suck, squeeze, bang, blow just as the engineers intended so you always get the result you want. And here's how it works. The ECU is connected to an array of sensors and the software uses the feedback to monitor the actual performance of your engine against pre-set criteria, in this case the optimum performance level the design engineers expect from your engine. The ECU then sends you visual and auditory information about what's going on inside your engine via the dials, gauges and lights on your dashboard and you use this information to make your driving decisions. And as you know, how you drive dictates how easily you get to your destination.

Mmm, OK got that too, but what's that got to do with me?

Now substitute think, feel, act, for suck, squeeze, bang, blow and tell me what that conjurors up in your mind.

Not quite sure to be honest, you'll have to clue me up.

Here you go, think, feel, act describes the internal process we guys go through when we decide to do something and we need to create the power and drive to get it done. Just as your engine goes through suck, squeeze, bang, blow everytime you turn the key, we go through think, feel, act every time we hit the start button. And for us guys the process works like this, how you think dictates how you feel and how you feel dictates how you act. And, as you already know, it is your actions that dictate your results.

Mmm, reminds me of a line from that Troggs song "My minds made up by the way that I feel" I think Wet Wet Wet did

a version of it too.

And again, just as with your engine, the process is controlled by the software programme you have loaded on your ECU, the piece of technology that sits between your ears. Your ECU is connected to your five senses, sight, hearing, touch, smell and taste and it's through your senses that you collect data about your world, data which you then use to monitor and make decisions about what's happening in your world.

And here's how the process works. Your senses collect the data and filter it through the software on your ECU to give it meaning and value against pre-set criteria, and the criteria here is the performance level you currently believe you can achieve. The meaning and value you give to the data may be positive or negative but the important fact to be aware of now is that it is the feedback you receive from the filtered data that you use to make your decisions as to which course of action to follow. And as you know, it is your actions that will determine your results. And, just as you are familiar with the dials, gauges and lights on your car's dashboard you will recognise the feedback from your ECU as the voice in your head and what it says to you, the pictures you create and see in your minds eye, when you decide something is or is not to your taste, when you smell a rat or sniff an opportunity and ultimately how you feel about an idea.

OK, I can see how it works so what's next?

Here's something to think about, either behind the wheel or steering your course through life you are the driver, it's your hands on the wheel so you are the one in control. It might not feel like that right now but just as you learned the process for driving your car so it takes you where you want to go you can learn the process for driving your life so you always get to where you want to be. And here's how the process works. If you want to get more suck, squeeze, bang, blow from your motor you take a trip to the garage where the technician plugs it into his magic box and with a few clicks of a mouse he re-maps the software on the ECU and you drive away with more power and greater performance than when you drove in. And here's some more good news, the process works just the same way for you. You can learn to re-map the software on the ECU between your ears and the result of your mastering that skill will be an increase in your personal power and performance that will soon become evident in every aspect of your life.

OK, I hear what you're saying and much as I'm happy with how some things are there are others I'm truly sick and tired of and really want to change so I'm open minded to hearing more.

Sounds good to me and here's the opportunity to do just that, and remember, it's not just about keeping pace you can use the skills you're learning now to put yourself ahead of the game.

Mmm, I get it and that's at least three new ideas I've collected and I'm starting to feel a buzz inside me now. So what do you call this new methodology I'm learning?

The full title is Neuro Linguistic Programming which you'll find defined in the textbooks as "The study of the structure of subjective experience and what can be calculated from that". But that's not as important right now as you knowing what the technology can do for you.

And that is to reveal to you how you create your own version of the world from how you think about the events that occur in your life. And why is knowing that important? The answer is, from knowing that you will find it easy to master the skills you need to take control of your think, feel, act process and drive your life in your chosen direction.

To complete the picture here's a snapshot of the origins and evolution of NLP. The technology was co-created by Dr. Richard Bandler who identified the skills and devised the techniques that will guide you through making the changes you want a part of you as you continue your journey through this book.

So you can see how all the parts fit together and the whole system works let's break it down into its components. Neuro refers to how your ECU gathers data about your world, which is through your senses so you have five input channels which feed data directly into your ECU where it is processed by your nervous system. Linguistic refers to your verbal and non-verbal communication systems through which you code and attach meanings to the data you collect. And remember, voice tone and body language are important components of your comms system because how you say something and the physical picture you present communicate meaning as much as the words you use, as the saying goes, a picture is worth a thousand words. Programming refers to the process of how you create your individual perception of the world. Having already attached meaning and value to the data you've collected you then use the results to create a master reference programme, which you store on your ECU, and it is this programme which you use to direct your behaviour and, as you know, it is your behaviours, your actions, that will ultimately determine your results.

OK, I get the idea, getting the right result is all about running the right software on my ECU so I'm no longer a passenger but now I'm the driver and in control. So where do I find the right software?

That's one of the skills we'll be learning, how to organise your data and comms systems to develop programmes that deliver the results you want, and a good place to start is familiarising ourselves with how what is now came to be because this will give you a solid foundation on which to build. And as you continue through this book a good way to view it is as a manual, the purpose of which is to help you learn the skills you'll need to get what you want so you can enjoy a smooth journey to your Promised Land and with that in mind feel free to refer back to it any time your suck, squeeze, bang, blow feels in need of a tune-up. And an important point to note here is that, just as a when you're working on your motor, the manual can explain how to swap a water pump or seal a gasket but it is only by you doing the job that you really master the skills of how to do it.

3

Who Do You Think You Are?

You are the only person who knows everything about you, many may know your name but only you know all your secrets, what you really think and how you feel. But, have you ever asked yourself how you came to be the you who's actively reading this now? You may find yourself asking why that matters and the answer is simple, it's because your thoughts become actions and actions become habits and your habits will determine your results. So with that in mind lets chunk down a level and start with an explanation of what's going on inside you now, because as you gain a deeper understanding of how the mechanics of your internal process, your suck, squeeze, bang, blow works you'll begin to notice the improvements and as you start seeing the results for yourself you'll feel like you're making real progress.

Picture the scene, you'd noticed her earlier as you scanned the room and your man brain kicked-in with its instinctive snap judgement and told you that on its scale of two you'd definitely give her one. Now you see her again, standing all alone, her friends gone to the bar for more Pinot Grigio and gifted you the chance to smooth on over. So what you gonna do? Some guys don't hesitate they just stroll on over and start playing the game while others hesitate, to weigh-up the situation and before they know it her friends back with the drinks and the opportunity has been lost. So which was it for you, green for go or wait on amber? Whichever choice you saw yourself making you'll recognise both and so can recall times in your life when you followed your instinct and ran with it, and only afterwards, if ever, paused to question your reasoning, and equally times when you hesitated, unsure of your next move, times when you literally felt in two minds so you put yourself in neutral to consider your options. And being able to recall the times you went with your gut and the times you hesitated leads us to the question of why do we do that, react instinctively in some situations and find ourselves in two minds in others?

OK, You got me there, I guess it's to do with that think, feel, act and "my minds made up by the way that I feel" thing, sometimes my gut says go for it and sometimes I'm not so sure so I start looking for the catch.

Good answer, now you're really starting to rock. It's because your ECU is made up of two minds, your conscious mind and your sub-conscious mind.

Your conscious mind is the part of your ECU which pays attention, and thinks logically, working out that when faced with a no-entry sign if you take a series of right-hand or left-hand turns you can then drive up the road that leads you to where you want to be. It is the part of you that decided what make of car and which house to buy. Insurance industry statistics show there are more fender benders in the summer months and their explanation for this is based on the fact that your conscious mind can only focus on one thing at a time. Their reasoning is that as the temperature rises women wear fewer clothes, which we men find a most pleasing distraction, but it causes us to shift our attention from the road ahead to the delights of the passing female form so we end up driving forward but with our eyes looking to the side and the result is we have a fender bender. And they aren't wrong, but the part they missed was that most guys believe the main purpose of their rear-view mirror is so we can check out the best examples from both sides.

While your conscious mind is busy awarding marks to passing females your sub-conscious mind is working much harder and doing a much bigger job than most of us realise or give it credit for. Why don't you have to consciously remind yourself to breathe? It's because your sub-conscious mind performs a number of tasks for you automatically, one of which is controlling your body's functions and so it keeps you breathing without you having to remember to do so. Such is the power of our sub-conscious mind it can automate even seemingly complex tasks and so we perform them as though we are on autopilot. Recall the times you've driven yourself home from work or the shops and not remembered the journey? The journey is familiar and so we let our conscious mind wander and trust our sub-conscious mind to repeat an action we have carried out many times before. And again insurance companies say this explains why the majority of car accidents occur close to home.

In addition to keeping you breathing your sub-conscious mind performs a host of other functions for you. It is the home of your memories, your habits, your creative skills and your beliefs. You can think of it as your combined trip computer and sat-nav. It records your memories of where you've been, all that you saw and heard on your journey and how you felt about the trip.

If I say recall times when you felt really good about yourself your sub-conscious mind will automatically begin to search through all the memory data it has stored about the times you felt really good about yourself and as it locates each one it passes the file to your conscious mind so you can re-live those pleasurable moments now. Your habits are simply an automatic repetition of an action you have taken many times before and as time passes they become more and more ingrained in your psyche and eventually you reach the point where you don't recall hearing the bell but you still answer the call. In each familiar situation your sub-conscious mind automatically directs you to follow the same route all over again without you having to think about it. It works just the same as when you make a selection from the Previous Destination screen on your sat-nav, it got you there before so you hit the button and without further thought you follow the same directions. Habits illustrate perfectly what are often referred to as unconscious patterns of behaviour and given how common these are it's surprising that jumping to conclusions and the rush to judgement are not yet Olympic sports.

Remember when you sat up all night looking for a solution to a problem and then it suddenly dawned on you? That was your sub-conscious mind being creative. All the time it was beavering away in the background searching through what you knew about the problem and all that you could use to solve it and as it came up with each new idea it sent the file to your conscious mind to make you aware of it so you could assess your options and act on the best one. It's just the same as when you're trying to drive somewhere and you run into a traffic-jam, you hit the Find Alternative Route button on your sat-nav, it takes a moment to assess the options and having done so it gives you a new set of directions that allow you to get to your destination by navigating a path through or around all the obstacles.

You've got somewhere to be so you jump into your car and tap the postcode into your TomTom and, as it calculates the route, the voice alerts you to any potential hazards you may encounter along the way, anything from road works to low bridges to toll charges or speed cameras. Now take yourself back to the bar we visited earlier, the one where you had the chance to smooth on over and try your luck with the girl whose friend had gone to the bar for more Pinot Grigio. Remember the question we asked, why do some guys see the green light and jump straight in and others wait on amber? The second half of the answer is that your sub-conscious mind has an in-built radar designed to protect you by alerting you to any potential hazards or danger and here's how it works. Guy walks into a bar, sees the girl, his sub-conscious radar gives him the green light and he's straight over there ready to deliver his best lines. The alternative is guy walks into a bar, sees the girl, his sub-conscious radar flashes up a warning like a light on the dashboard and so he hesitates while he tries to figure out what the danger could be, he's not instantly sure but he recognises the feeling he gets when his radar says be alert so he waits as his conscious mind tries to figure it out. Finally it dawns on him why the light was flashing, memories of a previous experience, the last girl he met there turned out to be a bunny-boiler and the last thing he needs is another one of those.

OK, I'm with you now, there are two parts to my ECU and each has their own job, the conscious part pays attention and asks questions and the sub-conscious part is where I store my data, just like a hard drive. Thinking about it I guess the reason men never hesitate to totty watch when driving is that we all feel safe in our cars.

Right on the first point, could be on the second one. Anyway, now you know how your internal process, your think, feel, act, works and all the good things your sub-conscious mind does for you but it's also important to be aware of another characteristic of your sub-conscious mind and that is the fact that it does not make value judgements.

When you ask your sub-conscious mind to retrieve some data for you it will collect the last file you saved on the subject and pass it to your conscious mind without questioning its value relative to your current aims, and as you know this data will ultimately dictate your actions and results. This can lead to problems and here's how the problem works. We've all heard the stories about people getting stuck in narrow lanes or driving into deep water as they blindly followed the directions from their sat-nav and only later do they realise the reason for their misfortune was that they had failed to update the maps stored on their device to the latest version and so the device had based all its calculations on corrupt reference data. And it works exactly the same with the sub-conscious mind, if we blindly follow the information it gives us without first checking for updates then our journeys may not be as smooth as we would like. And so, as we motor on, the question to ask now is what reference data does your sub-conscious mind use to direct you? The answer is your beliefs. And if you baulked at that statement it is because you do not believe it to be true! To get the full picture lets take a look at how the process flows from end-to-end so you can get a feel for how and why your beliefs have such a massive impact on what you will or will not attempt to do. Your ECU combines all the beliefs you have acquired to create your very own individual map of the world, a map which serves as the master programme you use to pinpoint your position in the world. Faced with a challenge you go inside and check your map for directions and this starts your think, feel, act process. And it is the feedback you receive at the end of the process that will determine which course of action you follow.

From understanding the impact beliefs have on our lives let's chunk down a level and ask where do our beliefs come from? Some are given to us by well-meaning people we trust, like our parents, teachers and friends, and some we learn from our experiences, and often a one-off experience can create a lifetime of belief. And let us not forget the neg-heads who delight in sharing their bad beliefs as to what others are capable of achieving but can't explain how they know. Your personal values will also influence your beliefs, and if you want to clarify what your personal values are you'll find a free download on my website, but there are no laws that say living your life according to your values and reaching your Promised Land are incompatible. If anything the opposite is true, just think of the people who have achieved success because they came up with new ways to improve the lives of others so you can feel free to live a life based on your values as you achieve success. Here's a quick exercise that will show you how acquiring and accepting beliefs can be a passive process, how once acquired the tendency is to store them away for future reference and rarely if ever question their current value. Think of a belief you hold because somebody told you it was true and a belief you hold as a result of your own experience. Now ask yourself when you last questioned either of them?

OK, warning understood, like whoever it was said "If you do not ask a stupid question you'll do a stupid thing"

I like that, might even use it myself. And here's how it unfolds from there, you may currently believe that reaching your Promised Land is not possible for you, but ask yourself, how do you know? The answer is that you cannot be 100% certain because without questioning it you cannot be 100% certain that the belief is correct. It took Thomas Edison ten thousand attempts to perfect the electric light bulb so even if you have attempted something in the past and did not get the result you wanted, circumstances may have changed. So ask yourself once more, how do you know? That was then and this is now and many things may have changed in your favour since then but as you have not questioned your old belief you are yet to become consciously aware of them.

We've covered a good few miles and now it's time for a pit stop. And for all your efforts and all you have learned you've earned the right to feel good about yourself. And this is not the first time you've felt good about yourself so access your inner sat-nav and from the Previous Destination screen select another time you felt good about yourself and return to it now and see what you saw, hear what you heard and feel how good you felt and as you enjoy that feeling of feeling good notice where you feel it in your body and as you locate that feeling give it a colour and let that colour wash over you from the top of your head to the tips of your toes. Keep the good pictures and sounds in your head as you squeeze your thumb and index finger together as you concentrate on the good feeling of feeling good as you repeat the process five times.

Now take a moment to recall the model and colour of the first car you ever drove and having done that squeeze your thumb and index finger together again and notice how when you do this the good feelings of feeling good about yourself come back.

OK, Done that and I can feel it working but gotta say I'm intrigued as to how it works.

It's one of those simple but brilliant fixes, a short-cut to feeling good. Squeezing your thumb and index finger together as you concentrate on the feeling of feeling good creates a positive association which is then stored on your ECU. So now everytime you want to have that feeling just squeeze your thumb and index finger together as you concentrate on the feeling of feeling good. And if you want to give yourself an extra boost make the pictures bigger and brighter, turn up the volume and speed up the feelings in the direction they are moving and feel terrific now.

4

Have You Checked Your Head's Straight?

Right, that's our pit stop completed and with fresh rubber on each corner now it's time to get back on track. We've seen how our beliefs are a powerful driving force in our lives and how we seldom, if ever, question them. Indeed, as we will see, the reality is we spend more time looking for evidence to support and reinforce them than we ever do questioning their validity. The way we do this is a by-product of how your ECU processes the mountain of data that you encounter every day and the reason this is important is because how we do this is largely a sub-conscious process but the consequences will be real so it's probably a good idea to understand how the process works.

OK, I'll go along with that, I never realised there was so much going on in the background. It's fascinating really and I'm starting to get the feeling there's a whole load of untapped power there.

You ain't wrong, and here's how it works. In every waking moment our senses are collecting data and because we lack the processing power to consciously keep tabs on it all we have developed a set of filtering mechanisms to deal with it and prevent our conscious minds from becoming swamped. Our filters are the systems we use to decide on the value of the data and what meaning we attach to it and a key point to be aware of here is that as we filter the data it stops being objective and becomes subjective, because we all have our own individual filter settings, and these settings are based on our current beliefs as to what is and what is not true. You then use this filtered data to either reinforce or update your personal map of the world, the map you store on your ECU, the one which will determine your suck, squeeze, bang, blow, and ultimately how smoothly your journey goes.

There are three filtering mechanisms we use to manage our raw data, deletion, distortion and generalisation and now feels like a good time to look at how each one works.

Let's head back to our favourite bar and watch Mr Green in action. He's noticed the girl and as her friend went to get the drinks he sensed his opportunity to smooth on over and make his move. At that moment the only things that existed in his world were him and her and the world of possibilities that making her acquaintance would open up. Sure there were other people around but not in his world, he had deleted them from his picture, his focus was on the opportunity at hand and so for Mr Green deletion worked in a positive way. Mr. Amber, on the other hand, had deleted the memories of the many good times he had enjoyed playing the mating game and chose to focus on his one not so good experience and so for him deletion worked in a negative way because now he will never know.

A woman decides she wants to get fit and asks her husband if he will work out with her. He's happy to help and puts together a programme that he knows from experience will take her where she wants to be. As a man, his ECU loads up his "If we're gonna do this, we're gonna do it right" programme and so he focusses on the importance of good technique. They start their work out and the man, at the same time as praising his wife's efforts, offers a few pointers as to how she could improve her technique explaining that not only will this prevent injury but will also get her to where she wants to be much faster. Mrs does not take too kindly to the advice, in her mind she has distorted his good intentions into a criticism of her and so she put's on a face like a smacked arse and gives off that "no chance of a shag for you" vibe. And from that you can see how distortion can work in a negative way. The good news is that after a little explaining to clarify his intent Mrs gladly accepted his help in the spirit it was offered and now has a body to die for and Mr is happy too as he is now on a promise. Check out this quotation from Johnners commentary on the 1976 Test Match between England and the West Indies and you'll see the positive side of distortions, "The bowlers Holding the batsmans Willey"

It's holiday time and you're off to the sun, you drive to the airport, park your car, jump on the plane and look forward to a relaxing time by the sea and sand. You clear customs and pick up the keys to your hire car, it's not the same make or model as the one you have at home but without a second thought you jump in, fire her up and hit the road. A car's a car, what's to think about, manual or auto, you know how to drive so you just do it. This is a generalisation, the third of your filtering mechanisms, in action. A generalisation is where we create a one-size-fits-all belief about something, we learn to drive and we then generalise that as all cars work the same we can easily drive any car we choose. Believing that you can drive any car on the planet is a positive generalisation that sets you free, as long as there are cars available you will always be able to get around easily. Problems occur when we generalise a one-off bad experience into a rule, rather than treating it as the one-off event it was, because this leads us to create a belief that there will always be a negative outcome in those circumstances. And that is why Mr Amber found himself in two minds, he had generalised his one bad experience into a one-size-fits-all belief that he could no longer safely enjoy a spot of totty watch in that bar.

OK, I see how it works, Mr Green and Mr Amber both filtered

the data they collected but their filtering only succeeded in reinforcing their original beliefs about what could happen next.

Spot on, as Thoreau said, "It's not what you look at that matters, it's what you see" And what this reveals is, the truth is an illusion, an illusion we create for ourselves and it is based on our current beliefs. Mr Green and Mr Amber were standing in the same bar at the same time, looking at the same situation with the same intention but when they went inside and checked their maps Mr G saw a highway free from stop signs leading straight to his Promised Land and Mr A saw a highway jammed with roadworks that stopped him in his tracks. And what that also tells us is that the right illusions work well for us and to further illustrate that fact just overlay a London Underground map with a London street map and you will discover that the station layout as shown on the Underground map bears little relation to the physical geography found at street level. Alight at Bond Street station and you will find yourself on Oxford Street, a five minute walk from where the map led you to believe you would be. This is because the Underground map is an illusion, it's a schematic diagram used to represent the system and was designed to show the relative positions of the stations along the lines rather than their actual geographic positions. Yet despite this fact millions of people are happy to believe in the illusion of the London Underground map and trust it to help them navigate their way around the Capital. And, because now you know the truth is an illusion, you can clearly see the value of questioning your beliefs because, just as with the Underground map, your internal map is not the physical territory it is just your personal representation of it.

OK, I get the point. I'm sure I read somewhere that people told Ray Kroc people wouldn't eat burgers sitting in their cars and Walt Disney that there was no future in a cartoon mouse

with big ears. I guess if Ray and Walt had just accepted those beliefs without questioning them today there would be no McDonalds and no Mickey Mouse. I guess the doubters are on-board now.

Spot on, the reason that we have McDonalds and Disney World is because Ray and Walt not only questioned conventional thinking but each created for themselves a strong belief in the value of their ideas and an equally strong belief in their ability to bring their ideas to life. And the good news is it works just the same for the rest of us guys and here's some more good news, the next thing you're going to learn is how to create a strong belief in your ability to reach your Promised Land.

A good place to start is by parking your old belief and opening your mind as you take a look around you now to see what new information you can collect that will help you on your way because better quality information gives you more and better choices, so you make better decisions which stacks the odds in your favour massively increasing your chances of success. Logic will take us so far but as you know, from watching Mr A compete with himself, beliefs operate at the sub-conscious level and so to build that strong belief you need to go deeper to make those changes and an easy way to do that is to take an MOT test. Not the Ministry of Transport one that you have to put your motor through every year but a Modus Operandi Test that will show you how you do it now and reveal to you how you store your strong beliefs on a different part of your ECU from your lesser beliefs and you already know the impact your beliefs have on your suck, squeeze, bang, blow process. And with that in mind let's hit the road.

MOT- Modus Operandi Test

Let's start with a simple baseline test to uncover where on your ECU you store your strong beliefs and where you store your lesser beliefs so you can see how the process works for you. Use the parts list, you'll find it at the end of the chapter or you can download one from my website, to collect the data about your feedback, noting the location and tone of your internal voice, the pictures you see in your minds eye, taste and smell data and the physical sensations you experience. Chunk down to capture the fine detail, your submodalities, of each of your senses. If you can see yourself in your pictures, just like watching a movie that you are starring in, this is called disassociated and if you cannot see yourself in your pictures, because you are seeing the event through your own eyes, this means you are associated.

Start with a belief you hold strongly, a good example is, do you believe that a Ferrari California will be faster from 0-60mph than a Ford Mondeo? As you consider the question fill in the details on your parts list gathering as much data as you can.

Now consider another question on which your belief is not as strong, it may be, do Vauxhalls hold their value better than Fords? Again, as you consider the question fill in the details on your parts list gathering as much data as you can.

Now compare the two results and notice the differences. Become aware of your submodalities, how do the voices sound different, are the images of different sizes or colour, where are the voices and pictures located and how do the sensations differ from each other?

Having completed your MOT you will understand how your ECU is organised, how your good feelings of belief and certainty and the lesser feelings of uncertainty are located at different parts of your ECU. And here's some more good news, this new understanding will give you more torque and traction and accelerate the change process making it even faster and easier for you to get the results you want, because that understanding is all you need to build a big and strong belief that you will get to your Promised Land. So let's put the pedal to the metal and get the party started by learning to use the Swish Pattern. Practise makes perfect and repetition is the mother of skill so practise using the Swish Pattern until you feel comfortable using it. You may find it helps to start with changing a minor, long held belief such as, will I always bite my nails? and build up from there as your confidence grows and you see how creating good strong beliefs translates into positive actions and positive results.

Belief Change Technique – Swish Pattern

1 Think of a limiting belief you no longer want to have – For example, that you will have the problem for a long time or the rest of your life.

2 Think of a more resourceful belief that you want to have such as being free from the problem now and for the rest of your life.

3 Study the submodalities of certainty and uncertainty that you have noted on your parts list noticing their differences.

4 Vividly imagine firing off the limiting belief you want to be free from into the distance and it rebounding back from the horizon into your submodalities of uncertainty.

5 Simultaneously vividly imagine firing the resourceful belief you want to acquire into the distance and it rebounding back from the horizon into your submodalities of certainty.

6 Repeat five times quickly as you feel the changes becoming part of you.

OK, I get it, having a strong belief that I can succeed is key and creating that strong belief really comes down to a question of data management. All I have to do is decide which strong beliefs I want and use the Swish Pattern to load them

on to the right part of my ECU and then run the programme and go with it everytime.

You got it, remember back to when we talked about what NLP will do for you and now you have a perfect illustration of how it works. It's all about aligning your suck, squeeze, bang, blow so your thoughts, feelings and actions support your objectives and that all comes from your holding a strong belief that you can.

And while we're on the subject you will also have discovered why NLP works really well for all of us here in Man World, it gives us the power to create new solutions to old problems without the need to bare our souls or talk about how we feel. Our focus is on how the the feeling works, how the process flows, what comes first, the voice or the images, because that is what created the feeling. The event itself is neutral, it only becomes good or bad when you stick a label on it. When you know how the feeling works you can just decide you want to change, identify how you want to change and use your tools to create a programme that delivers the result you want. And the really good news is that you can do all this in the privacy of your own head.

Now it's time for a pit stop. And for all the resourcefulness you have added to you you've earned the right to feel confident in yourself and your future. And this is not the first time you've felt confident so access your inner sat-nav and from the Previous Destination screen select another time you felt confident about yourself and return to it now and see what you saw, hear what you heard and feel how good you felt and as you enjoy that feeling of feeling confident notice where you feel it in your body and as you locate that feeling give it a colour and let that colour wash over you from the top of your head to the tips of your toes. Keep the good pictures and sounds in your head as you squeeze your thumb and index finger together as you concentrate on the good feeling of feeling confident as you repeat the process five times.

Now take a moment to recall the model and colour of a car you would like to test drive and having done that squeeze your thumb and index finger together again and notice how when you do this the good feelings of feeling confident come back.

OK, I'm doing it, I got used to doing that to feel good so I guess with both loaded I'll feel good and confident at the same time.

Right on, we call it stacking anchors and you'll find that when you combine the two it more than doubles the power of one. So now everytime you want to have that feeling of feeling good and feeling confident just squeeze your thumb and index finger together as you concentrate on the good feelings. And if you want to give yourself a turbo boost you can make the pictures bigger and brighter, turn up the volume and speed up the feelings in the direction they are moving and feel your motor run. The trip is on.

Suck, Squeeze, Bang, Blow – Parts List
Sub-Modality Comparison

PICTURES	CERTAIN	UNCERTAIN
Moving / Still	....	....
Size	....	....
Shape	....	....
Colour / Mono	....	....
Sharp / Blurred	....	....
Bright / Dim	....	....
Location – Left / Right / Centre	....	....
Bordered / Borderless	....	....
Flat / 3D	....	....
Associated / Disassociated	....	....
Near / Far	....	....

SOUNDS	CERTAIN	UNCERTAIN
Volume	....	....
Pitch	....	....
Mood	....	....
Tempo	....	....
Tonality	....	....
Duration	....	....
Rhythm	....	....
Location – Left / Right / Centre	....	....
Harmony	....	....

KINESTHETIC	CERTAIN	UNCERTAIN
Location In Body	....	....
Tactile Sensations	....	....
Temperature	....	....
Pulse Rate	....	....
Breathing Rate	....	....
Pressure	....	....
Weight	....	....
Intensity	....	....
Direction Of Movement	....	....

SMELL & TASTE	CERTAIN	UNCERTAIN
Sweet	....	....
Sour	....	....
Bitter	....	....
Aroma	....	....
Fragrance	....	....
Pungent	....	....

5

With The Sports Pack & Full Leather?

Money in the bank, a big house, wired for sound and vision and in the right location, a German motor or two parked on the drive and climbing to the top of the corporate ladder. All sounds great and if you ask people to define success it comes as no surprise if their answer is to offer you a similar list of goodies, a list of material stuff that society has generalised into being evidence of success. In this game the rules are simple, the more stuff you acquire the more success points you score and he who scores the most wins.

Now ask yourself, is the game really that simple? Accept the rules as they appear and we leave ourselves with only one narrow definition of success, how much stuff we amass. This also suggests we all want the same things and leaves us with only one way to measure success and that is by comparison with others, you just tally up your stuff and work out your place in the success league. Advertisers spend millions of pounds interrupting our favourite TV shows to promote this model of success. They seek to convince us that if we share in their illusion of success, the one where you gotta have their latest must have, then happiness will be your reward. So, if we follow that illusion then surely the boys with the most toys would always be happy, because, under the rules of the game, they won. And equally the guys with the least stuff could never be truly happy simply because they just do not have enough stuff. Then you switch on the news and find the illusion is somewhat shattered by the stories of guys with loads of stuff who get themselves mixed up in all sorts of mad capers and who, when asked to explain their actions, say it was because they were unhappy with their lives. And, on the flip side, there are an equal amount of stories of guys who live a minimalist life and are blissfully happy.

OK, I guess maybe there's more to this success thing than first appears.

Could be so let's motor on and see what we find. Suck, squeeze, bang, blow, the trip is on and you're on the way to the Promised Land. Remember back to when we first started out and how, as you heard yourself say I believe in the Promised Land, your mind filled with the images of all that you will have when you arrive and notice now how holding this thought again brings your senses to life once more as your movie plays technicolour pictures of how it's gonna be flow through your mind as your inner voice lays down a rocking soundtrack over-dubbed with dialogue that lets you know this is success and as you feel your body come alive with excitement the feeling tells you this is real and this is now. And as you tune-in to your feeling of success notice which comes first, the soundtrack, the movie or the feeling because the order in which your senses ignited tells you how you "do" the feeling of success and so now you will recognise it again and again in the future. And being aware of how you "do" the feeling you understand that success is as much a feeling on the inside as having a babe magnet parked on your drive on the outside.

And from here you can just accept that feeling or go a little deeper now and uncover the underlying emotion to that feeling, is it the satisfaction of knowing that you did it or is it the peace of mind that comes from knowing that you did and so you can again and again long into your future? Whichever tag you decide to attach to your success feeling will be personal to you because it is your feeling and from learning how you "do" success comes some more good news. And that is the knowledge that our subconscious minds cannot tell the difference between a real and a vividly imagined experience, remember the times you woke up after a vivid dream and had to ask yourself, did that really happen? It's a part of you and all of us and one that we will be making full use of and turning to your advantage as we continue our journey.

OK, I'm with you, I kinda knew there was more to it than just stuff. And the working out how I "do" the feeling part reminds me of the way Formula1 drivers use simulators to learn all the different circuits so they arrive with a game plan that suits their driving style.

Spot on once again, and just as the F1 guys check their telemetry for specific data to see what can be learned, so they can fine tune their plans, you can climb back into your simulator and as you re-live your success feeling begin collecting the new data that will fill in the blanks and accelerate your progress. You've already got a clear picture of which motor you'll be parking outside of what style of home, along with all the other material rewards your success will bring you, so now notice what you see yourself doing to fill your days because doing this now will reveal to you your instinctive choice of how you want to live your life. At this point some guys feel a gentle nudge, largely happy and content they would like to climb one more step on the promotion ladder but only because the pension's bigger. Other guys notice a massive shift as their instinct leads them to a new road and they become aware of the feeling that screams to them "This is what I was born to do" and they feel driven to achieve more as they realise they have found their purpose in life and the strength of the feeling makes it impossible to ignore. You're a practical man and you're wise enough to upside and downside a plan as you look for ways to make it happen and you already know the cost of not doing is always more than the cost of doing because the biggest regrets are for the things we never did and the short cut to peace of mind is living a life with no regrets so the feeling cannot be ignored.

OK, I'm there, it's just like Amelia Earhart said "Courage is the price that life extracts for granting peace" I guess we've all got a role to play but it's up to us to make it rock.

You got it in one and now as your sub-conscious mind starts working on your plan in the background let's check in with Mr Green and Mr Amber to see how they're doing. Mr Green looks like he is making solid progress, his start point was to ask himself three simple questions, what do you enjoy in your life and want more of, what do you not enjoy and want to let go of and what new ideas do you have to fill the space? He then checked in with his feelings so he felt sure about the decisions he'd made as to the rewards he was chasing and his chosen path to securing them. To the naked eye it appears he has had a trouble free journey, and largely he has, and if you ask him to share his secret he's happy to oblige. Knowing what he wanted he went inside to ensure his suck, squeeze, bang, blow was perfectly aligned with his objectives. By doing this he knew that regardless of whatever obstacles he encountered his think, feel, act process would support him and lead him to finding a solution. Smooth as it looked Mr Green's road was not entirely without bumps, the most memorable one came as he sought to explain his plan to his nearest and dearest. Top of his list of motivations was to create a better life for those he loved and so, having picked what he felt to be the right moment, he say's "Hey Honey, let me tell you about my new plan" In a flash the atmosphere changed as Mrs G shot him that look that say's "There can't be a plan if I wasn't consulted" Fuck, he thinks, now I'll have to explain why I didn't mention it before as well as explaining the plan. Thankfully, just like you, Mr Green is a practical man and had thought about how it would affect Mrs G and the cubs and so had calculated the time and other resources he would need to invest to make it happen so explaining his plan was the easy bit. Now Mrs G is fully on-board, she just needed a little time to run the data through her ECU to get comfortable with it, and now she's happy with the plan Mr G is nearly forgiven for not consulting her earlier. No surprises there, we already know things work differently in Girl World. What do girls and cars have in common? Both are occasionally going to give you trouble and both need a regular service to keep them tip-top.

Checking in with Mr Amber we find he too is making real progress and, just like you, we find Mr Amber doing success his own way, he's even given it a name, calling it "My Brand of Normal" because he knows we all do things a little differently. To the outside world his progress may not appear rapid but Mr Amber chooses to do things at his own pace, he likes to look at things from every angle and so affords himself the time he needs to feel he has got a rounded view. Mr A's start point was just as Mr G, working out what he wanted more of, what he wanted less of and how he'd fill in the gaps. As he went inside to align his suck, squeeze, bang, blow he uncovered two issues he felt merited further investigation because that way he could be sure his think, feel, act would be fully in tune with his objectives. The first was the impact success would have on his life and those of his kin. Being a thorough man Mr A decided to dig a little deeper and was surprised to find this was a common thought, often referred to as fear of success, and if left unreconciled, had been known to stop guys in their tracks. To Mr A the answer was simple, he knew that success wouldn't change him, because he liked who he was, and his objective was to change his circumstances not his character. And knowing this he felt secure that his important relationships would not be adversely effected. The flip side of the coin was fear of failure and again Mr A decided he needed to better understand how that works. He understood that fear is just an emotion and, as is the case with all our emotions, one we create inside us and from there he could see that fear is just the result of an out of tune suck, squeeze, bang, blow or to put it another way, an out of tune think, feel, act. But more importantly Mr A realised that his new skills made him the master of his emotions and so there was nothing to fear. Indulging his passion for going deeper Mr A decided to check out how some of the great and the good from history had handled the emotion we know as fear of failure and that's when he remembered our old friend Thomas Edison and the story of his success journey. After ten thousand attempts Edison finally perfected his invention and became the first man in history to have a light bulb moment. With a clear objective in mind Edison saw value in each attempt that did not deliver his desired result, viewing the outcome not as failure but as feedback. And it was this feedback that created the opportunity for him to gather new data, data which gave him more and better choices as to what to try next. Hence Edison saw himself as a man who dared to dare, a man who never quit and whose endeavours would ultimately benefit all men and he believed that this reflected positively on him as a man. As he enjoyed his own light bulb moment Mr A exclaimed aloud "If that strategy worked for Thomas Edison then it will work for me too" Feeling good at this point Mr A chuckled as he mused that if the England football team learned the Germans penalty taking strategy would the shoot-outs last longer and would England finally win one?

Now it's time for another pit stop and as you hit your mark take a moment to check your toolbox and see that it contains all the tools you need to overcome any obstacles you may meet on your journey and enjoy the peace of mind that comes from knowing you have all the tools you need to enjoy success again and again long into your future. You know your purpose, it's what you were born to do, you know what you want and how you're going to get it and how good you'll feel when you do. And, knowing this you recall success is as much a feeling on the inside as having a babe magnet on your drive on the outside. And this is not the first time you've felt successful so access your inner sat-nav and from the Previous Destination screen select another time you felt successful and return to it now and see what you saw, hear what you heard and feel how good you felt and as you enjoy that feeling of feeling successful notice where you feel it in your body and as you locate that feeling give it a colour and let that colour wash over you from the top of your head to the tips of your toes. Keep the good pictures and sounds in your head as you squeeze your thumb and index finger together as you concentrate on the good feeling of success as you repeat the process five times.

Now take a moment to recall the model and colour of the first car you ever owned and having done that squeeze your thumb and index finger together again and notice how when you do this the good feelings of feeling good, feeling confident and feeling successful come flooding back.

OK, I'm doing it, we're really stacking the anchors now. I'm feeling good, feeling confident and feeling successful and that's everything I asked Santa for last Christmas.

Right on, and remember three more than doubles the power of two and you can still add a turbo boost by making the pictures bigger and brighter, turning up the volume and speeding up the feelings as you feel your motor run. And while you do that I'll fire up the DeLorean because next time out we're going back to the future.

Suck, Squeeze, Bang, Blow

6

Time To Hit The Road

Money in the bank, a big house, wired for sound and vision and in the right location and a German motor or two parked on the drive. Still sounds like a whole heap of great stuff and again if you ask people what their goals are it's no surprise when they tell you their goal is to acquire loads of great stuff. And there's nothing wrong with that. Anyway, have you ever heard of a fella called Lao Tzu?

Yeah, wasn't he the guy from way back when who first asked the question "Is it better to give a hungry man a fish so he can eat today or is it better to teach him how to fish so he can eat everyday?"

He sure was and the smart answer remains the same today as way back then. So as we motor on to look at goal setting let's stick with the wisdom of Lao Tzu and set your goals as learning and using new skills so they become an integral part of you, and we'll refer to all the cool stuff using those skills will bring you as rewards.

OK, works for me. As Einstein said, the definition of insanity is "Doing the same thing over and over again and expecting different results" and anyway, I've never been fishing before!

And the good news is that this method will work for every guy who makes the smart choice and making the smart choice here is key because it is only positive actions that will produce positive results. It's a simple process so let's take a look at how it flows. Actions are behaviours and it is by taking actions you encode the skills into your master programme on your ECU where they become a part of you. Doing this both increases your resourcefulness and automatically updates your personal map of the world. The end result is that the next time you need to use that skill your sub-conscious will deliver it to you automatically at precisely the right moment. In short, you now possess the skills, it's your hands on the wheel so you're in control and now you can use your skills all the time and reap your rewards everyday. So, now you know what you want and you've set your goals to learn the new skills you'll need to get your rewards, the question is what's the easiest and simplist way to begin acquiring those skills? And the answer is to use a skill you've already started to master so fire up your simulator, jump in and let your imagination flow because we're going back to the future.

This exercise is just like taking your motor for a full service. We're going to clean up any niggles hanging around from your past, like that squeaking spring, top-up your fluids to keep everything cool and check your geometry to ensure your wheels are balanced and aligned so you stay on-course to your Promised Land.

Think about time and notice where you see the future, is it ahead of you with the past behind you or is it to one side of you with the past on the other? Now you know how you mark time and as you see your timeline stretching out use it to plot your course as you begin to fill in the details of your action plan. Now think about time as we know it and you'll see it does not really exist. Time as we know it is a man made system, an illusion, but we are all happy to share the illusion because it allows us to collectively organise our worlds. We check our watches and the relative positions of the big hand and the little hand tell us when to start and stop, how long before the game kicks off and how long before we need to be home if we want to avoid grief. So if time does not really exist what are we left with? The answer is moments, the here and now, and the speed of your progress will be determined by how you choose to fill each moment so take a moment now to complete this exercise and as you do feel free to stand up and move around if that works better for you.

Your Timeline

1 As you look at your timeline mark where you see the present moment. Step up to that mark and start the future just behind your eyes so you are active in the here and now with your eyes on your future. If the past is behind you, leave it there and if it's to one side of you nudge it back so it's just over your shoulder.

2 As you look along your timeline put in some reference points, your last birthday and your next birthday and the moment you will claim your first reward will work.

3 Float up and back above your timeline to your earliest memory and as you float back to the present moment enjoy again all your good memories as you put them on one side and without giving them a second thought put all the challenges on the other side. Give each side a colour if that works better for you.

4 Again float back above your timeline to your earliest memory and as you travel back to the present take a moment to enjoy all your past successes bringing with you all the resources that created your success and push away and behind you all the challenges bringing with you only the good lessons you learnt so you never make the same mistake again.

5 As you stand in the present notice how your past has

changed for the better now and how resourceful and prepared you feel to execute your plan for your future.

6   Take this good feeling with you as you float into your future to the time you will arrive in your Promised Land and mark the moments at which you will take all the action needed to secure your victory. As you see yourself taking action and making progress notice all that you did and how you got it done and as all this is happening feel your body vibrate with motivation, the fuel that powers your engine, as you see yourself power your way along the highway of success.

7   Return to the here and now and see yourself taking action through your own eyes like an actor in a dress rehearsal. Seeing is believing and so feel your belief growing ever stronger because now you have seen the proof with your own eyes. You knew what needed doing and now you know that you got it done and so right now is an excellent moment to fire off your anchor stack.

8   When you arrive at your moment of victory pause for a moment and look back and see again what you did to win and spin that success feeling faster and faster taking your rev-counter to the red-line and know you are firing on all cylinders now as you feel your body vibrate with motivation and excitement.

9   As you hold on to that feeling come back to the present and look again into the future and notice how your future has changed, see how it has become bigger and brighter and how you as a man of action can see your way past, through, over or under any challenge that may arise as you take your next positive step on your trip now.

OK, I got it, I use my timeline to create and refine my action plan. I work out what skills I'll need, practise them in my

simulator to iron out the bumps, and then I'm ready to hit the road and get the job done.

Got it in one, and remember to refer back to it everytime you're planning your next move to ensure you stay on track because when you control your preparation you control your performance and so you can feel confident of getting the result you want. And with that in mind let's catch up with Mr Green and Mr Amber to see what they have learned from going back to the future.

Mr G reports that having taken a fresh look at his past he now knows there's no such thing as unfinished business. He now happily accepts that whichever way it went the best thing about the past is that it's over and says this realisation has left him free to focus his thoughts fully on getting where he wants to be. Mr A, to satisfy his liking for going deeper, added in a step and applied the SMART test to check that his goals were specific, measureable, attainable, realistic and that he had set a definite timeframe for making it happen. Satisfied that his goals were right for him, Mr A found that after reviewing his past he was able to separate the learnings from the old feelings and that by doing this he found he was able to forgive himself for any past mistakes. With eyes on the future Mr G and Mr A, although very different characters, both commented how completing the exercise had shifted their focus to their futures, increased their motivation to master the skills they would need and cemented their belief in their ability to get the job done.

OK, I'm right there with them. Looking out to my future I feel like I can see for miles and my motivation and belief are running red hot.

And this is not the first time you've felt motivated to learn new skills and put them to work for you, I'll bet that learning to drive is another one of those times, so access your inner sat-nav and from the Previous Destination screen select another time when you felt motivated and return to it now and see what you saw, hear what you heard and feel how good you felt and as you enjoy that feeling of feeling motivated notice where you feel it in your body and as you locate that feeling give it a colour and let that colour wash over you from the top of your head to the tips of your toes. Keep the good pictures and sounds in your head as you squeeze your thumb and index finger together as you concentrate on the good feeling of motivation as you repeat the process five times.

OK, I added motivation to my anchor stack and now everytime I squeeze I feel this smooth, rapid acceleration just like I'm shifting up through the gears at exactly the right revs.

And you'll also find that all those good feelings will combine to load a new Action programme on your ECU and that squeezing again and again in the future will give you a short-cut to the feeling that you can and that you have and will automatically spur you to further positive action. And if you want to increase your suck, squeeze, bang, blow you can add a little nitrous to the mix by making the pictures bigger and brighter, turning up the volume and speeding up the feelings.

7

Be Lucky

Ever bought a lottery ticket?

Yeah, loads over the years.

Ever believed you'd win or even expected to?

Not really, it's down to the luck of the draw so the best I can muster is hoping to win but I'm not banking on it.

You've hit the nail on the head there, the sort of luck you need to win the lottery is outside of your control, all you get to do is pick your numbers and hope. And it works the same way for everything guys take a punt on when they're betting on an outcome over which they have no control. We pick a horse or bet on how many goals a team will score and hope that our horse or team does the business for us. At least with tossing a coin we can stack the odds a little because we can choose which side is facing upward before we toss it.

Like I say, I buy a ticket but I'm not banking on it but I'm interested to see where we're going with this.

Right on. Some guys see luck as just a matter of chance, some guys even walk around with the belief that they aren't blessed with luck but others say you make your own luck in this world so I thought we'd take a look at how the suck, squeeze, bang, blow of luck works and, who knows, maybe we'll all start being lucky.

OK, works for me but I'm still buying a ticket if it's a rollover.

No worries. So we know there's no skill in winning the lottery and if we had mastered the skill of beating the bookies on our other bets there wouldn't be any more bookies so either there's no skill in it or we just haven't worked it out yet. So what about making our own luck in situations where we do get to influence the outcome? If we can find the skill in that, and we all learn that skill, then we can all walk around believing we really are a bunch of lucky fuckers after all.

OK, that definitely works for me.

Consider this quote from Johann Wolfgang von Goethe, I think he found the secret to making your own luck and was kind enough to share it with the rest of us.

"Until one is committed, there is hesitancy, the chance to draw back, always ineffectiveness.
Concerning all acts of initative and creation, there is one elementary truth the ignorance of which kills countless ideas and splendid plans:
That the moment one definitely commits oneself, then providence moves too.
All sorts of things occur to help one that would never otherwise have occurred. A whole stream of events issues from the decision, raising in one's favour all manner of unforseen incidents and meetings and material assistance which no man could have dreamed would come his way.

Whatever you can do, or dream you can do, begin it.
Boldness has genius, power and magic in it. Begin it now"

And there you have it, our old mate Goethe found the secret and showed us all that the skill needed to create your own luck is being committed to achieving your purpose and backing your commitment with positive action. And, so you can see how the Lucky process flows from end-to-end, let's give it a quick run through. As you know your ECU is constantly collecting data about your world, data which you then filter, so some of it gets deleted, some distorted and some generalised and your filter settings are based on your beliefs. From the work you have already done you know what you want, you have begun mastering the skills you'll need to get it done, you've created your plan and committed to following through with action and most importantly, you have built everything on a big strong belief that success is your destiny. And the good news is that your holding that belief has automatically re-calibrated your filter settings so now you see a different map, your headlights are on, your antenna is up and your radar is automatically scanning the world for opportunities that will lead you to your Promised Land. In short, because you are committed to your success and taking positive action the process of creating your own luck has become automatic for you and so you already qualify as a lucky fucker.

OK, I'll go along with that, I definitely feel everything is on the up and my world has changed for the better.

And this is not the first time you've committed to getting the job done and got the feeling that events were suddenly working in your favour so you know what to do next.

OK, let me guess, add the feeling of being born lucky to my anchor stack.

Right first time so take a pit stop to do that now and when you've added feeling lucky to your anchor stack squeeze your thumb and index finger together to fire-off your anchor stack and take a moment to enjoy feeling good, feeling confident, feeling successful, feeling motivated and feeling lucky and then we'll motor on.

8

A Full Tank Of Juice

You've filled the tank and kicked the tyres, you know what you want and how you're gonna get it so everything in your world looks, sounds and feels great. And as you take a moment to enjoy feeling great notice that you created all these changes from the inside and that they have become a part of you now and put you fully in control of your life. In the past your conscious mind wasn't always aware how resourceful you really are but now you understand how to marshall your forces, how to tune your suck, squeeze, bang, blow, your think, feel, act so it fully supports you you can clearly see the simple truth that all the resources you will ever need to reach your Promised Land already exist within you.

OK, I get that. I feel I can safely park any doubts here now because I know that, whatever the challenge, I have the tools to create solutions that work for me.

Right on, and now you've put yourself firmly on the highway to success let's take a look at how you can use your new skills to accelerate your progress so you arrive in your Promised Land ahead of time.

As you will recall the textbook definition of NLP is "The study of the structure of subjective experience and what can be calculated from that". Well, the good news is that one of the things that can be calculated from that is how other guys tuned their suck, squeeze, bang, blow, their think, feel, act to achieve the result they wanted. And the doubly good news is that you can import that model into your world and, with maybe a little fine tuning, make it work for you too. Mr A showed us how this process works when he adopted Edison's strategy for dealing with those times when a man's efforts do not immediately deliver his desired results. Rather than quit Mr A followed Edison's lead and took the learnings from his efforts and got ready to go again. And with that in mind let's take a look at the challenges that try to sneak up on us here in Man World and the successful strategies other guys have used to defeat them because then you can put your tools to work for you and innoculate yourself against them.

OK, I get that too, when I'm faced with a challenge there's no need for me to reinvent the wheel, instead I can just look at how successful guys tuned their suck, squeeze, bang, blow and use my tools to tune mine the same way.

Exactly, and because your new way of thinking is already a part of you that means you can always keep your engine running smoothly and sounding sweet.

9

Easy On The Throttle

See if you can fill in the blanks in this story. Harry has not been feeling his best, finding himself short on patience and struggling to hold everything together as he tries to function despite feeling that he is permanently at boiling point. It's as if his thermostat is set too high and so he finds himself constantly in danger of overheating. He's tried telling himself to cool down and be more patient but things just don't seem to be improving. Not wanting his Missus to feel the cause was something she'd done he explains how he feels and tells her that he has also developed a rash, which to add to his woes, has now started to itch. His Missus suggests a visit to the Doctor may be a good idea, if only to get some cream for his rash, so Harry updates his Boss and leaves work an hour early to see what can be done. Next morning his Boss is not surprised when he get's the message "Harry won't be in for a couple of days, the Doctors signed him off with a _____ related illness"

Er, stress?

Correct, got it in one, and given what a popular diagnosis this is today it's probably a good idea for us to understand how the suck, squeeze, bang, blow of stress works.

OK, I'll go along with that.

Check a medical dictionary and you'll find stress defined as the arousal of your autonomic nervous system. Go a little deeper and you find that stress, which is also known as our fight or flight response, is far from being a modern invention but has been with us since our caveman days. Back then, before supermarkets and take-aways, we were all in the hunting business and so we would grab our clubs and spears and leave our caves to hunt for food. As we stalked our prey we knew that we too were being stalked, by wild animals who viewed us as dinner, and as both predator and prey, we quickly learned when to stand and fight and when to run away. Sensing danger our in-built radar would sound the alarm and automatically trigger our fight or flight response and such was the success of this system in protecting us that it became hardwired onto our ECU as our automatic reaction to challenging situations. And clearly, back in the day, having a stress response was a positive as it ensured you didn't get eaten when you went out for something to eat. Unaltered by evolution our fight or flight response, that feeling which today we know as stress, remains hardwired onto our ECU and continues to work exactly as it always did. Sensing danger your ECU automatically triggers your fight or flight response and begins releasing testosterone and adrenaline into your system and pumping extra blood to your muscles as it prepares your body to fight or run away. And an important point to note here is that as your heart pumps extra blood to your muscles the blood flow to your brain is reduced and this explains why guys may find it hard to think straight when they feel under pressure. So, now we know that our stress response is a positive legacy from our caveman days the question is what changed to create todays negative view of stress? And the answer is, the times we live in and the circumstances in which we feel stress.

Here in the 21st Century our stress response still has a positive role in Man World. It's unlikely you will ever have to outrun a wild beast but it's good to know that if you face a challenge and need to raise your game your ECU will automatically release a shot of adrenaline to boost your performance. The downside of our stress response can be seen in those times when we we perceive a threat but are denied our options of fighting back or taking flight. When the Boss is growling, we're stuck in heavy traffic, there's too much month left at the end of the money or we've had a row with the Missus, in short, any situation where you feel the urge to stand your ground and fight back or just put the pedal to the metal but feel denied either option. And from that list you'll notice another key change, the type of perceived threats that trigger our stress response have changed. Gone are the physical threats of wild beasts to be replaced by threats to our self image, our ego. And another important point to note here is that your ECU doesn't make that distinction, it treats all threats the same, and so it triggers our fight or flight response and we feel stress. And knowing this it's our job to make the distinction between positive stress and negative stress and to do that we need to recognise where and when we get the feeling.

OK, I'm with you there. Looking at it now I can see the difference between good and bad stress and it's easy to see how negative stress can lead to anger and frustration.

Top stuff, and now we know the difference I guess it would be a good idea to find ways to manage negative stress and with that in mind let's take a moment to check in with our buddies Mr G and Mr A so they can share their experiences of negative stress and what they did to control it.

Mr G reports that he used to feel negative stress when he felt others weren't keeping pace with him. It could be at work, where he liked things done quickly, but didn't always take the time to make sure his instructions were fully understood, or out driving when he could never understand why some people insisted on stopping at roundabouts when, from his position behind them, he could clearly see there was no traffic approaching from the right.

Mr A says his experience of negative stress was most pronounced during business meetings with one particular colleague. Being a thorough fella Mr A had mapped out where the process began and ended and saw that it began when the meeting popped up on his diary and ended as he left the meeting. He couldn't be 100% sure as to the guy's motivation, to him it felt like the guy was abusing his position to dump on him, but regardless he was pleased with his findings because now he knew how the process worked. Experience had taught both Mr G and Mr A that there will always be times when practical considerations would deny them the option of walking away or fighting back and this knowledge led both men to the same conclusion, a level of negative stress is inevitable. And both being practical men, they realised that if they were denied those two options the smart move was to create a third option. And that was to find a way to manage their negative stress, because this would give them back control so then they would always find those times much less stressful in the future and that put them one step ahead of the game.

Mr G found what worked best for him was a technique called One Point which comes from the martial art Aikido. Using this technique Mr G found it easy to control his stress response and this gave him the time and space to be able to think clearly, because he now felt calm in situations that used to wind him up, and so he was able to get his message across much more effectively. And the nett outcome for Mr G was not only did he feel happier in himself but his results also improved. What Mr G loved about this technique was that it was the same one the little guy in kung-fu movies used to prepare himself to walk calmly into a room full of heavies and proceed to systematically lay them all out and rescue the girl. And so each time he uses it Mr G feels just like a Ninja warrior, completely in control on the inside whilst appearing serene on the outside because now those situations trigger feelings of relaxation in him and bad stress has become a thing of the past. And so you can discover how well the One Point technique will work for you here is a step by step guide for you to follow.

Aikido One Point Stress Control Technique

1 Think about a task or situation you found stressful in the past and give it a stress score, 1 being very low stress and 10 high stress.

2 Put your feet flat on the floor and shift your conscious attention to your belly-button and locate a spot about half-way between your stomach and your back as you ponder which way your belly-button swirls.

3 As you notice the soothing feeling of peace, calm, tranquility and inner strength that washes over you think about that task or situation again and notice how the thought of it feels less stressful now.

4 As you feel the muscles in your body relax repeat the exercise until the thought of the task or situation registers only a 2 or 3 on your scale. Leaving it as a 2 or 3 will ensure you have enough energy to deal with the task and are fully in control.

5 As you enjoy this feeling climb into your simulator and run through the task or situation seeing everything going perfectly before you return to your endeavours feeling refreshed and reinvigorated.

Mr A used to look at his colleague and wonder if the guy really was some kind of dickhead or if that was just his perception of him but, more importantly, what he did know for sure was that he created his feelings on the inside and that meant he could master a technique to control them. And the solution Mr A mastered not only allowed him to control his response but also stripped his tormentor of all of his power leaving the poor guy puzzled as to what had changed for Mr A. And, again, so you can discover how well the Donald Duck technique will work for you here is a step by step guide for you to follow.

Donald Duck Exercise

1. Think about that person who causes you bad stress and make an image of them looking at you in the way that they do when they cause you bad stress. Hear them saying their usual nonsense and notice where the bad feeling happens in your body and where their voice is located.

2. Now make this image black and white, shrink it down and as you move it off into the distance put a clowns big red nose on their face.

3. Hear them saying what they usually say but hear them say it in Donald Duck's voice, or Micky Mouse's if you prefer.

4. Notice how this makes you feel differently. Take a moment to hum or sing the first verse of your favourite song and think of them again and notice that you still feel differently about them.

OK, I get it, whatever the trigger, be it a particular place or a certain person, either one of those techniques will take the sting out of it.

Exactly, and just to keep you fully up to speed, Harry's been on the phone to share what the Doc told him about stress. He covered the fact that an element of negative stress is inevitable and that the smart move is to master some stress control techniques, the Doc's mantra is "If you control the stress you'll avoid the related illness" The Doc also said that our bodies automatically store energy to feed our fight or flight response, just like having a Mars bar in the glovebox in case you get hungry, and added that we need to find a way to burn off this excess energy because doing so will increase our stress capacity so you will feel less stress in the future. Doc says physical exercise is the way to go and that if H doesn't fancy joining a gym he could try brisk walks, jogging, cycling or for about £30 you can get a skipping rope and a set of dumbells in Argos so you can do a simple cardio and weights workout at home. The Doc gave him the once-over to check he was OK to exercise and told him half an hour three times a week will do nicely and to use the other days for rest and recovery.

OK, I see the Doc's point, get out in the fresh air and work up a sweat to burn off your stored energy and you'll be doing yourself a double favour as you'll increase your stress capacity and get fit at the same time. H's Doctor sounds like a top man, I don't suppose he gave H the Argos catalogue numbers for the kit?

I didn't ask but it's good to hear you sounding so chilled and I'll bet this is not the first time you've relaxed completely knowing that you're headed in the right direction.

OK, let me guess what comes next, I add the feeling of being completely relaxed to my anchor stack?

Spot on, and as you do notice now how feeling good, feeling confident, feeling successful, feeling motivated, feeling lucky and feeling relaxed have become a total part of you. And this has happened because each time you squeeze your thumb and finger together as you concentrate on the good feelings you strengthen the association and this has created new thought circuits on your ECU. It's just like driving over a patch of grass, the first time you do it you can see your tyre tracks and as you continue to do it the changes become more and more noticeable and then you notice you have created a whole new road and now you automatically follow that road because you know it will take you exactly where you want to be. So take a moment to update and fire your anchor stack now and then we'll motor on.

10

Running On Empty

Here's a question for you, what is it that can affect any of us guys, is said to collectively cost us £9bn per year and led Doctors to issue in excess of 50 million pill prescriptions in 2014?

Here's a clue, guys will often describe their experience as "I felt I had the weight of the world on my shoulders" or "It was like I had a dark cloud hanging over me" or "I felt paralysed and unable to move" And here's another clue. The catalyst for this experience is often a major change in a man's circumstances, or indeed worrying about a potential change that may never happen. These changes tend to be events such as trauma, bereavement, redundancy, domestic strife or reaching a milestone birthday.

Er, depression?

Right first time. And given that it could creep up on any of us at any time maybe it would be a smart move for us to get clued up on how the suck, squeeze, bang, blow of that feeling we label depression works because once we understand how it works we can devise a practical solution to it.

OK, I'm all for that, when you know what you're dealing with it's always easier to find a solution.

Lets start by getting a handle on what depression really is and that's not as simple as it sounds. Check with a Doctor and you'll find that the diagnostic criteria is so vast that almost every guy on the planet could qualify and then ask a sample of guys what the term means to them and you'll likely get a different response from each.Talk to guys who say they are depressed and ask them this one simple question, "What, all the time?" and the most common answer is "No, not all the time, only when I think about X" Umm, so maybe what they really mean is that there are good things in their life and "X" is just the part they'd like to improve? And what this reveals to us is that there is no agreed definition. And so, because there is no agreement as to what depression actually is, the term has become distorted into a generic term that can be applied to almost any negative feeling. And, going a little deeper, if we can't agree a definition how can we know if we've really got it or that it even exists? At least with the common cold that endless stream of snot confirms the diagnosis.

So, because we're looking for practical solutions, let's start with what we know for sure, and the first thing to notice is that all the guys used sensory terms to describe their experience. They were describing how they feel or felt and that's our first clue. We know how our Man process flows - think, feel, act - and what this tells us is that the guys had to first experience some stinkin' thinking otherwise they would not be feeling the feelings they describe.

OK, that makes sense, it's logical when you think about it.

So the next question to ask is what caused their stinkin' thinking? And here let's make a distinction between the guys who label their experience as depression because they are trying to get somewhere and find themselves stalled or in limp-mode, and guys who label their experience as depression because they have recently been through one of life's major events. And the reason for making the distinction is twofold. Firstly, only you know the direction you are coming from and secondly, although both processes share common mechanicals, the differences tell us that the catalyst, the root cause of the issue, can be either a slow burn or a sudden impact. And, regardless of which direction you are coming from, the good news is that you will find that in your toolbox you already have all the tools you need to get yourself back on track. So, sticking with what we know let's move on and get the job done. We know that in both cases the process started with stinkin' thinking and we know that stinkin' thinking is the direct result of the feedback we receive when, as we start to plan our next move, we go inside and check our map for directions. And we also know that our maps are personal to each of us and reflect our beliefs.

To illustrate how each of these processes work Mr G and Mr A have kindly agreed to share some stories from their past so you can see what you can learn from them.

Mr G has a story about a time he was struggling to keep up with the demands he made on himself, and interestingly, he says he only really understood the process he had gone through when he used his timeline to re-code his past, as the exercise allowed him to keep the learnings but leave the negative feelings firmly in the past. Mr G had taken on an ambitious plan and finding that his progress was not as rapid as he desired he found that stinkin' thinking had begun to darken his view of his world and this led to feelings of frustration and increasing self doubt. The change was evident in the questions he began asking himself, he had switched from asking himself "How can I get this done?" to "Can I do this?" and the changes he was feeling on the inside were now being noticed by the people around him. And it wasn't long before a well meaning soul offered the suggestion that maybe he should label what he was experiencing as depression and so he should visit his Doctor. Mr G, as a typical bloke, baulked at the idea of visiting the Doc and felt doubly put off because he wasn't at all enamoured at the prospect of taking happy pills. Finding himself with limited options Mr G decided his best course of action was to do his best to ignore his negative feelings and get stuck in with the hope that things would improve. Knowing what he knows today, Mr G says that he would have immediately understood the reason he felt in limp-mode was just a simple question of faltering belief caused by slow progress and he would have known the solution was to give his suck, squeeze, bang, blow a tune up. And knowing this he would have immediately grabbed his Swish Pattern from his toolbox to create a big strong belief in his ability to deliver before using his timeline to refine his action plans and then donned his Ninja suit and got back to kicking butt. Knowing what he knows now Mr G is positive he never was depressed at all and that the root cause of his negative feelings was simply his frustration at his lack of progress.

Mr A's story relates to a life changing event he experienced. Mr A was busy enjoying life, he knew where he was going and had a firm plan for how he was going to get there. And then the phone rang. Wham, in one short moment Mr A found that his world changed, changed from a being a happy place where the future was bright to one where the dark clouds of despair filled the sky. Now his feelings were confusion and sadness and despite his best efforts he struggled to focus on even mundane, routine tasks and the thought of pursuing his life's purpose weighed heavy on him and left him feeling like he was trying to climb a mountain without a rope. Each time he tried to focus he found his mind bouncing back to the event as his inner voice posed probing questions like Did that really happen? How did that happen? What more could I have done? If I had done X would it have changed things? And as the questions kept on coming those around him also became aware that things had changed for Mr A and, not surprisingly, he too was given the suggestion that perhaps the event had left him depressed and maybe he should visit his Doctor. As well meaning as his friend was, Mr A shared our Man reluctance to visit the Doc and instinctively felt that the general approach of dishing out antidepressants was not the best answer for him. Mr A felt that this was his challenge and so required a solution that worked for him and he decided that taking a systematic approach to the issue was the best route for him.

Logic had always served him well in the past so he set about using the tools he had collected and applying what he had learned to create a solution that worked for him. He knew that if he could map the process he was going through then he would also automatically uncover his underlying emotions and because he now understood how his emotions worked, and how to manage them, he knew this would help him to find peace of mind again. From his own experience Mr A could see how major events provoke an emotional response in us and how this can impact our state of mind. And as he mapped the process he could also see there was a tendancy for the associated negative feelings to spill-over and become generalised into other parts of our lives and how this seepage could in turn cause us to perceive the event as having had a negative impact on the whole of our being. And with this realisation Mr A revealed clue number two, because we perceive the event to be life changing this new belief alters our maps and the changes are reflected in quality of the feedback we receive from our ECU.

From this Mr A realised that what he had been experiencing was the natural process of coming to terms with a major event, it was the beginning of his recovery and definitely not depression. Knowing this Mr A understood that it was a natural part of the healing process for questions about the event to occasionally come into his mind and he viewed taking a moment to answer them as a practical, worthwhile task because it allowed him to feel secure that he had done all he could reasonably have done and he knew that resolving his feelings of confusion would lead to enlightenment. Mr A also understood that the time this took would depend on how many scenarios he felt needed to be addressed and the good news is that as he answered each question for the last time and filed it away, separating the learnings from the feelings just as Mr G had done, the questions became fewer and fewer and he noticed his life was getting better and better. In short, by applying what he had learned Mr A was able to clearly understand the experience he was going through and give himself a tune up from the neck up and get back on the road to his Promised Land.

OK, got that. Listening to our buddies stories I can see that depression is really just a label people tend to stick on any bad feelings so it's always a good idea to dig a little deeper because then it's easy to work out what the real challenge is and overcome it.

Spot on, the key is finding the reference point, the experience that started the process, and you can think of it like this. If your motor starts blowing blue smoke the chances are the fault is not with your exhaust but is to be found earlier in the suck, squeeze, bang, blow process. So when you take it to the garage the technician will look for where the fault begins, it maybe a blown head gasket or an oil leak, and that's where he'll start to make the changes to put things right.

And it's worth remembering that the start point may have been a real life event or the result of a guy misusing his simulator and creating a bad experience in his imagination, because, as we know, our sub-conscious mind cannot tell the difference between a real life and a vividly imagined experience.

And because we're all practical guys let's be thorough and acknowledge that there can be other times in our lives when we may feel like we're not firing on all cylinders. Such is the popularity of labelling feelings as depression it's worth noting what other factors may leave us feeling a little sluggish, factors that have more to do with our 21st Century lifestyle than a major change in our circumstances. Poor diet, too much of a good thing, not enough exercise and not enough sleep can all impact our body chemistry and leave us feeling a bit flat and you can easily work out if you need to make any changes here.

And, with thanks to Mr G and Mr A, so you can discover how quickly you can unravel and understand any negative feelings you may have here is a step by step guide for you to follow.

Avoiding And Defeating "Depression"

1 Some guys get the feeling that they have never been happy and this is just the result of one bad feeling being let loose. If you ever find yourself here just switch on your inner sat-nav and select your third most happy memory and take a moment now to re-live that memory in glorious technicolour and remind yourself you have been happy before and you will be happy again and again.

2 If you find your think, feel, act is about to lead you down a dark highway pause for a moment and use your One Point tool to stop the process before the thought has a chance to grow.

3 As the soothing feeling of peace, calm and tranquility washes over you notice where the bad feeling began in your body so you understand how the process works and back up one step from there.

4 From there re-focus on your mind on your desired outcome and ask your sub-conscious mind to help you find new ways to achieve it and avoid the negative feelings and notice how you feel empowered as those new ways come into your mind now.

5 As your new solutions come into your mind now climb into your simulator to take them for a test drive. Start by watching yourself taking positive action and achieving the results you want, just like you're watching a movie, and notice which option gives you the best feeling and

that feeling replacing the old one.

6   Feeling comfortable and well rehearsed with what needs to be done step into the movie and see yourself taking the positive action through your own eyes, seeing what you'll see, hearing what you'll hear and feel how good you'll feel in your moment of triumph.

7   Revisit your timeline and as you float along it mark the points that show you when you will be putting your skills to work and the point at which you take the chequered flag to signal victory.

8   Fire your anchor stack and as you enjoy feeling good, feeling confident, feeling successful and feeling motivated remember your commitment is automatically bringing good luck rushing to meet you on the Highway to Success and begin taking positive action now.

OK, I'm with you, that one is like a multi-purpose tool, you could use it to identify, understand and negate any negative feelings you ever have. And then it's just like using your anchor tool in reverse, you back up to the step before the problem used to occur and change it so you never fire the negative anchor so you never get the problem. What I also noticed was that, although the guys were coming from different directions, neither Mr G or Mr A needed pills to solve their challenge.

Right on and big-up for you for spotting that. That reminds me of something Harry was telling me about his recent visit to the Doc. H said he asked about pills and the Doc said that, even with all the hi-tech brain scans they can do today, there is still no evidence that the feeling so often referred to as depression is related to a chemical imbalance and so the whole idea of using chemicals to treat it is questionable, particularly if all they do is mask the symptoms and leave the guy's problem unresolved. The Doc said he prefers to help people to work out where in their process the problem occurs, which also reveals the cause, so then they can back up a step and put the fix in before the problem occurs. Doc says that this approach works best for everyone because it puts guys back in control of their lives, saves us all money and frees up his time to help people who really need his expertise.

So far we've learned strategies for successfully dealing with feelings of frustration and the emotional impact of life's major events but there is one emotion that can, if left unresolved, leave guys stuck in the passenger seat and taken for a ride by their negative feelings. And that emotion is guilt, the root cause of which will be either something you did, to yourself or to somebody else, or equally something you failed to do, again for yourself or for somebody else. And with that in mind here's a simple method to put the matter to bed and regain full control of your life.

Defeating Guilt

1 If the root cause for you is something you did or failed to do for yourself take a moment now to forgive yourself for your error.

2 Look for ways you can remedy the situation by acting differently now and use your newly acquired tools to create an action plan and begin to implement it now.

3 If the opportunity has passed, as you consign the episode to the past for the last time separate the learnings from the feelings and feel good knowing you will never make the same mistake again and notice how doing this opens up bright new horizons for you.

4 As your new choices come to mind commit to a new direction and use your newly acquired tools to create a new belief and then update your action plan and begin to implement it now.

5 Create a new anchor to cement the changes into place by squeezing your thumb and second finger together as you focus your attention on your new direction seeing what you will see, hearing what you will hear and feeling the good feelings you will feel.

6 Take a moment to ask yourself what you fancy for dinner tomorrow and then fire off your anchor and notice how the good feelings come back.

7 If the root cause for you is something you did or failed to do for somebody else take a moment now to forgive yourself for your error and, saying the words aloud so you can hear yourself speaking, offer your apologies without excuses and ask them for their forgiveness.

8 Notice the feeling of peace and relief this creates inside you and as you consign the episode to the past for the last time separate the learnings from the feelings and feel good knowing you will never make the same mistake again and notice how doing this opens up bright new horizons for you.

9 Decide to do a good turn for a stranger, just something simple like letting somebody into the traffic or stopping to let somebody safely cross the road, because by doing this you put good karma into the universe and the universe will reward you by ensuring it flows back to you.

OK, I can see how that works. I've heard the Police say that when people confess to their crimes they often feel relieved to have got it off their chests. So I guess it's hard for a guy to have peace of mind when he feels he's transgressed and doesn't yet feel he has atoned for his sins.

I'd go along with that, and the good news is that now you've mastered the skill of how to put the fix in one stage before the problem begins you'll never put yourself in that position and that is one more thing you can feel good about.

Suck, Squeeze, Bang, Blow

11

Always Check Your Blind Spot

Here's a question for you. You're driving along and you notice that your temperature gauge has hit the red so what do you do, just ignore it and hope the temperature drops back to normal or find a safe place to stop and check your oil and water?

Er, stop and check the fluid levels. If you just leave it chances are it will get progressively worse and you'll end up with a seized engine.

I'd go along with that, and while we're on the subject now is a good time to look at how stress and those negative feelings that are often labelled as depression can get progressively worse if they too are left unresolved. And I'd say this is important not just for ourselves but so we can also be aware of what guys around us may be experiencing.

OK, I'm in, we're all citizens of Man World so it makes sense for us all to chip something in for the greater good.

Gets my vote. So, knowing what we know, it's easy to see how a man who is wrestling with unresolved negative emotions can end up feeling that all the fun and pleasure are gone from his world. And, with his engine already running hot, it's no surprise to find he feels he is in a downward spiral and things are getting progressively worse. And, with our man feeling he is at the mercy of his emotions, the spiral continues and often the next stage in the progression is self harm.

And so, as it is part of a progression, it's probably a good idea for us all to understand the suck, squeeze, bang, blow of self harm. And the first point to note is that self harm can take the form of a man inflicting physical injury upon himself or behaving in a manner that is likely to sabotage his career or home life. Secondly it's important to note that such feelings do not discriminate on the basis of age so they can just as easily creep up on a young guy who's looking to make his way in the world as a fella who feels his once promising career has stalled or an older guy who finds himself wondering "What the heck happened to me". And finally it's also important to note that, despite how it may appear on the surface, our man's behaviour is motivated by good intentions. Our natural Man instinct is to protect ourselves, as illustrated by our fight or flight response, and because us guys are not great at facing or discussing our emotions, even with ourselves, we look inside for answers to our problems and when we are already feeling in a confused state this can lead us to some surprising conclusions. Conclusions such as the idea that inflicting harm on ourselves may solve our problem or at least attract the attention of those who could help us without our needing to ask for help.

And so we can understand how this progression works our buddy Roland has agreed to share how his experience worked and how he learned to re-tune his suck, squeeze, bang, blow and get his life back on track. Roland had experienced all the negative emotions we have already discussed, together with their side effects, and had reached the self harm stage of the process without ever realising that he was going through a process. To him all his woes were separate and unrelated and he says he had reached the point where he had "kind of decided this is how I'm meant to be" Roland's eureka moment   came with the revelation that in fact all his woes were linked. As he mapped the progression he could clearly see how each negative thought both reinforced the previous one and led him blindly to the next and eventually to the action of self harm. Understanding now that he was in fact going through a process Roland found it easy to implement the solution we outlined in the previous chapter. He identified the start point of his process and put his fix in one step before the problem began so it never had a chance to develop. And of course, doing this realigned his map so now it gave him positive feedback and now his world is once again the bright happy place of his Promised Land. As Roland says, "Once you understand the rules of the game you'll soon be back to enjoying playing once again"

The final stage in the progression is where the feelings of confusion lead a man to question the value of living, the ultimate consequence of which is suicide. And again, the thought is motivated by a positive intent, the thought of leaving something negative behind or heading to a better place, but when you look at the facts you can clearly see that it is a flawed strategy, an illusion, because none of us know for sure what awaits us after this earthly life so there is no concrete proof that such an action will achieve its objective. And because almost 5000 of our brothers in the UK suffer this fate every year, that's 100 every week, the first thing to note is if you ever find yourself having such thoughts you know now that the smart move is to immediately pick up your phone and talk to a buddy, relative or The Samaritans or any support group of your choosing, all of whom will listen to your story without judging you and guarantee that your conversation will always remain confidential.

You'll be doing them a good turn, because their purpose is to help other guys, and also doing yourself a good turn because no man should ever take a major step without first checking, and maybe even double checking, that his information is completely up to date. And what new information will you find? That comes from the guy on the other end of the phone who, having listened to your story says " Hey, I know how you feel, I felt the same way so let me share with you what I found" And now you feel like you've had a light bulb moment, call it an epiphany if you prefer, you're no longer alone, there are other guys who felt the same way and, because they are still here to share their experience with you, now you know that there definitely are other solutions to your challenges. And knowing that means you are now in a position to help other guys and you being in a position to do a good turn for others proves to you that you have real value as a man, a valued citizen of Man World and you may just be discovering that now.

Ever had a bucket of Kentucky Fried Chicken? Even if you've never tasted the Colonel's secret recepie chances are you are aware of it but do you know how it came to be? The Colonel ran a little road side restaurant serving mainly, yeah you guessed right, chicken. Then the US government built Interstate 75 which re-routed the traffic and along with it most of the Colonel's customers. Fuck that, if the people ain't coming to the chicken guess I'll have to take the chicken to the people thought the Colonel and backing his idea with action he began to franchise his finger lickin' chicken. And how old was the Colonel when he started out on his new road? He was 65. And so, as you can clearly see for yourself, it's never too late to go again and win.

We have already seen how an unresolved emotional issue can send guys into a downward spiral and how that spiral can then develop a momentum that makes it appear to be outside of our control. So to get a better understanding of what emotions may cause a man to think about suicide lets bring in our buddy Emile Durkheim, a guy who has done a lot of research into the suck, squeeze, bang, blow of suicide because, again, when you understand how a problem works you can stop it by simply putting the fix in before it develops.

Having analysed his data, Durkheim came to the conclusion that a lack of social integration, that feeling that we have somehow become detached from society, was the most common reason that guys came to think about suicide. And the root of that feeling of detachment is based on a guy developing the thought that he is somehow failing to match up to the illusory stereotypical image of what a man should be. And, when we dig a little deeper, we can easily see how a guy can end up feeling like that.

A guy gets told that his JOB is now redundant but what he hears is that HE is redundant, and here you'll notice how the message has become distorted in his head. Where they said "JOB" he heard "ME", which his ECU automatically perceived as a threat to his wellbeing and so the distortion means he walks away from the situation experiencing negative emotions. Dealing with the practicalities of such a situation can be a challenge, there are still bills to pay and now the guy has to go through the process of finding a new job but the key point to remember is that despite his current circumstances he remains a capable, practical man. The change was in his external circumstances not his inherent worth and value as a man. And who knows what opportunities the situation may open up? The chance to re-train, learn new skills and pursue a different career or to strike out as an entrepreneur and start your own business. You only need to think big not start big, a sponge and a bucket is enough to start a window cleaning business and who knows how big it could get? Here in the 21st century the workplace is constantly changing so if you ever find yourself in that situation I guess the trick is to follow the Colonel's example.

Other well known side effects of struggling with emotional challenges include, insomnia, feelings of anger, reduced libido, giving ourselves a hard time and avoiding social events with family and friends. Add to these our Man tendancy to look inside ourselves for answers to a challenge we may not understand and our reluctance to discuss our emotions and you have an almost perfect recipe for isolation.

And here's how the process works, as we direct our attention inward in our search for solutions, we stop paying attention to the wider world and with our search proving fruitless the spiral continues and we become more and more introverted, further weakening our bond with the world. And here the paradox becomes clear, our natural tendancy to look within for answers can leave us feeling isolated from society but it is by participating in society that we express our individuality and work to achieve our purpose, and it is this which in turn allows us to assign positive value and meaning to our lives. And knowing this we can easily understand how the thoughts of a man who no longer feels congruent with his society can turn to questioning the value of his existence. And, having identified the suck, squeeze, bang, blow of suicide, Durkheim came to the conclusion that the causes have as much to do with how modern society works as it does the individual.

The good news today is that the growth of the internet has opened up new lines of communication and made it much easier to reach out and get help or connect with like-minded people and from there you can start to build a new life and re-establish your place in the world.

OK, I'm with you and now that us guys are starting to join together to raise our awareness about our mental wellbeing there is no longer any stigma attached to it because now we understand that it's a Man World issue and not an individual issue because shit can try to creep up on any of us.

Spot on. And education, getting all of us guys clued-up on the subject, is the key. Fact is shit is always gonna happen so what is really important is accepting that and being able to control your response to it, because then it stops being shit and becomes just one of life's challenges.

If we all learn to recognise the symptoms and understand how the problem works we'll be half-way there because it's always easier to fix a problem when you know how it works. And, add into the mix the knowledge that many of our fellow citizens who have been there will gladly share their stories of how they navigated their way back to happiness then we can all feel we can always move forward and go on to share our unique contribution with the rest of the guys. And if the voice in your head attempts to say anything different then notice the direction it is coming from and as you turn the volume control down to zero repeat aloud "Shut the fuck up" just as many times as you need to and as the voice disappears forever notice how the realisation that you are now firmly back on the road to your Promised Land cascades over you and congratulate yourself on a job well done.

Suck, Squeeze, Bang, Blow

12

Up For Another One?

Blip, blip, that's the car parked up for the evening and another working day done. Stepping into the house we hang our car keys on the rack and as our spouse updates us on the events of their day many of us indulge in a familiar ritual. And the question for you is can you guess which one?

Er, we open the fridge and reach for a cold one?

Right first time, it's part of the ritual many guys go through as their way of putting the events of the working day to bed and for most guys it works well. As the cold one starts to do its job they begin to feel relaxed and soon feel ready to turn their attention to domestic matters as they prepare to enjoy a relaxing evening at home. But for some guys the story takes a different turn and for them enjoying a cold one is not a step on the road to a relaxing evening but is the start of an endless cycle, one over which they feel powerless. And with that in mind now is a good time for us to check out the suck, squeeze, bang, blow of drugs and addiction. And fortunately H's Doc has offered to share his knowledge and clue us all up on the subject.

OK by me, he sorted H out so he sounds like he knows his stuff.

The first point the Doc made was he's not advocating we all become Monks, he was clear that there's definitely no preaching going on here, he's just going to lay it out and then we're all free to make our own choices. His next point was that all drugs, be they from your Doctor, dealer, off-licence, bookie or tobacconist, work the same way. He included bookies in his list because the absence of physical side effects means that guys often do not realise they have a problem until they find themselves financially ruined from chasing their losses and also because fixed odds terminals have been scientifically proven to be as addictive as Class A drugs. Doctors made the list because research in the USA has revealed that more guys are hooked on prescription drugs than heroin, crystalmeth and crack cocaine combined, indeed such is the scale of the problem that these drugs are now collectively known as Hillbilly Heroin and it's been said that their popularity has led to a fall in the price of street drugs as the dealers attempt to win back market share.

Doc then proceeded to explain exactly how drugs work. All drugs have been engineered to produce a change in your body chemistry and this change in your body's chemistry alters both your physiology, so you become aware of changing sensations within your body, and your psychology, so you start to think differently about the drug. And, so we can understand the psychological impact of drugs the Doc has given us two examples. The first example shows the psychological impact of prescription drugs, such as antibiotics, which have been prescribed to treat a specific ailment and the second example shows the impact of recreational drugs, which is 21st Century speak for the ones people get from their dealer, bookie, off-licence or tobacconist, together with prescription drugs such as psychoactives, that are used to treat psychological issues, and opioid analgesics, more commonly known as painkillers to those of us who are not in that business, that are used to treat post-operative and chronic pain and are often used long term.

A guy gets man flu and tired of coughing up grunge he bites the bullet and goes to see the Doc. He tells him what's up and gets a prescription for some antibiotics along with full instructions on when and how to take them and info about possible side effects because the Doc knows you won't read the leaflet. The Doc's a good guy and the only reason he gave you the pills was to free your body from illness and so you head off to the pharmacy content that the Doctor had your best interests at heart. You pop a pill and the grunge dries up, as time passes by the grunge returns so you pop another pill and once again find relief, and your doing this creates a psychological association between you feeling grunged up and reaching for a pill. The Doc gave you a week's supply, because he knows that's enough to get the job done, and you walk away happy because you had no intention of taking any more pills once you were cured. And so, with no worries in your mind there is no psychological legacy to deal with.

Doc did say that some guys view antibiotics as a panacea but when he explains they are not a magic cure for everything they just accept he knows best and walk away untroubled and let their man flu run its course.

OK, got that, I guess that explains all those unfinished packets of pills people have in their medicine cabinets, they start feeling better and so don't bother to finish the course.

Could well do. When it comes to recreational drugs and long term prescription drugs Doc says things work differently. With recreational drugs, because there are no underlying physical symptoms or pain to treat, the common reasons people start using them are to fit in with a peer group, find relaxation, self-medicating, or just experimentation. And with a massive choice and no need for a prescription the user picks which altered state they want to experience, be that slowing down, speeding up or a temporary state of stupor or euphoria, and head off to secure their drug of choice. Of course, in the absence of a prescription there is also no advice as to how long the user should continue to take the drug or what the side effects may be. Painkillers and psychoactives are initially prescribed to treat specific conditions and Doc says to understand their addictive nature we first need to understand how they work. And the way they work is by altering the brain chemistry of the user, they have been engineered to turn off receptors in the brain so the user is no longer capable of feeling pain, either physical or emotional, and noticing the change, in a very short time the user creates a psychological association between taking the drug and the absence of pain. Recreational drugs work in just the same way, they alter the brain chemistry of the user and so, in a short time they too create a psychological association between taking the drug and the feeling they are experiencing. And in both cases the user has yet to become consciously aware of the psychological link they are creating and they also remain unaware that the message contained in the link is the drug saying to them, as long as you have me every day will be a perfect day.

The Doc went on to reveal that the starting point for addiction is the moment the user becomes aware of the psychological link he has unwittingly created and that fear is the underlying emotion which   perpetuates the cycle. And here he shows us how the process works.

As time passes, the effects of the drug begin to subside and as the comedown feeling kicks-in the user becomes aware that his state has altered and this triggers his ECU to look for what has changed in his world. The realisation that the only change in his world is that he is no longer experiencing the feeling he gets from his drug activates the psychological link on his ECU and it automatically fires up it's "I Want More" programme, because it has learned that the quickest route to that feeling is to do more. And it is at this point the psychological effects of the drug reveal themselves to the user, through the tug of war now going on in the guys mind with the urge to do more pulling him one way and the question "What the hell am I doing?" pulling him in the opposite direction. And, as he attempts to make a decision on which way to go, fear steps in with an even bigger question which is "Are you sure you can get through life without me?" And, at this point with the guy already in a distressed state it is no surprise when fear overtakes him and he submits and so the cycle continues.

Doc says that it is usually at this point that guys start to become aware of the insidious nature of drug addiction and a subtle change occurs as they begin to see the reality of drug taking for what it is, slavery. Recreational drug users can see how the drug has created its own demand, there never was any underlying illness to treat and so the only reason they want more is because they took it the first time. And the guys who abuse themselves with prescription drugs, long after the original pain has passed, also realise that they have become slaves to a drug. And both guys live with the same paradox, they know that taking more drugs only perpetuates the cycle but fear prevents them from stopping. It's just like picking a scab, you want it to heal but everytime you pick it you prevent it from doing just that. And now they are both aware that their motivation for continuing to take the drug is not the same as the reason they took it the first time. Back then, at least they had a belief that there may be something positive to be gained but now they are fully aware that fear is their only motivation, fear of living without drugs and fear of going through the process of withdrawal. The good news is that having experienced the psychological and physical power of drugs they can now see through the illusion of guys having an addictive personality. Now they know the truth is that anybody who takes the drug could just as easily become addicted and from this they realise they are not a hostage to their personality and so can feel a sense of relief knowing that they can get free and resume their journey to their Promised Land.

OK, I get how it works, at first it feels like you're having a

good time and then suddenly you're having a shite time and you have to fight to get free. Sneaky stuff, it just kinda creeps up on you without you noticing.

That's how Doc tells it and he's the bloke who knows. And just like Doc said, there ain't no preaching going on here, what we're doing is helping guys who are struggling to leave an old habit behind to fully understand their problem so they can implement a practical solution and be free again. And with that in mind let's check back with Doc and see what course of action he would recommend to get it sorted.

Doc says there are two parts to getting free from drugs and addiction. One is dealing with the physical effects of having stopped using the drug and the second is unravelling the psychological effects of having used the drug. Doc adds that this is an important point to understand because as you begin your recovery you need to be fully briefed on what to expect, so you can view your experiences as positive steps on your road to freedom. Doc says that the physical effects of your stopping using drugs can be simply understood, what you are feeling is solely the effect of the drug leaving your body and that is why it is referred to as withdrawal. The time this process takes will depend on the drug involved but the important point to note here is that, with the passage of time, all traces of the drug will have completely left your body and taken with it all the physical effects of withdrawal. Doc says knowing this guys can clearly see that the physical effects of withdrawal are short term and at this point he offers a reminder that there are two parts to getting free and that the smart move is to always remember that so then you can separate the physical reality from whatever may be going on in your head.

Doc says that the process of getting free from the psychological effects of drugs and addiction begins with making a quality decision that you are going to get free now. He says that making this quality decision is what gives guys the steel and guts to see the process through because the first step to change is deciding that you want to change now. Doc emphasised that what he is talking about here is a quality decision that will give you back full control of your life and not a soft-soap decision where you decide to abstain for one day only to spend that day wishing it was tomorrow so you could get back to your drug. And with that in mind, the next exercise will help you to calibrate your suck, squeeze, bang, blow so you make a quality decision that will put you back in the driving seat by laying the foundations for your recovery and ensure you keep your rubber firmly on the road as you take all the steps you need to take to be free. And, as Doc said, what we're doing here is laying the foundations for your recovery and there are a number of organisations such as NA, AA or GA who can help you to build on those foundations. And remember, all those groups are run by guys who know exactly how you feel because they felt the same way and having come up with a practical solution they are more than happy to share what they have found with you.

And here's some good news, you already have all the tools you will need to complete this exercise in your toolbox so grab your parts list, roll out your timeline and fire up your simulator and lets get started now.

Good & Bad Decisions

1 Remember a time you made a quality decision in your life, one that has continued to deliver the results you want.

2 Use your parts list to collect the data about your quality decision. Note the location and tone of your internal voice, the pictures you see in your mind's eye, taste and smell data and the physical sensations you experience and chunk down to capture all the fine details.

3 Now use your parts list to collect the data about a bad decision in your life, one that had an unforseen and unwanted outcome. Compare the results of your good

and bad decisions and notice how the parts, your sub-modalities, are located in different places.

4 Think about making the decision to get free from drugs and addiction and as you record your feedback on your parts list check to see if the result fits with the location of your quality or bad decision submodalities.

5 Notice where you are in your addiction ritual as this will influence your state and hence your perspective. Often it is when an addict is without drugs, and so has to go through the hassle of acquiring more drugs whilst feeling the full effects of withdrawal, that they will see the benefits of getting free. Conversely, when they are in possession of their drug the only thing that matters is consuming more.

6 With that in mind, use your timeline to future test your result. As you look along your timeline way into the future notice what the outcome of your decision will be. Do you see a life where you got free and went on to achieve your purpose or is it one where you end up physically broken, mentally scarred and facing an untimely death?

7 And if it was the latter, ask yourself the question again and as you re-think the value of getting free do not not be surprised that it now fits snugly with the submodalities of your quality decisions.

8 Now you have made the quality decision to get free you have successfully laid the foundations for your recovery. And so now is the time to take positive action and contact one of the many organisations that will help you to complete and maintain your recovery.

9 Notice how making this quality decision has made you feel better already and notice the direction of that feeling inside you and spin it faster and faster so you are ready to take positive action right here right now.

OK, I get it, getting free starts with making a quality decision and immediately following it up by taking positive action because that will always lead to a positive outcome.

Spot on, and the good news is you can use this technique to sense-check all of your big decisions so you can feel secure that you have covered all the bases and you are on the right road.

Suck, Squeeze, Bang, Blow

13

Sex, Sex, Sex And More Sex

Sex, sex, sex and more sex, ooh yeah. From the first time he stirred and stretched out to reveal his full majesty you knew that your todger wasn't there just so you could take a leak. From that moment on the devil in your boxers has spent his time looking, hoping and praying for a yes so he can be let loose to show his prowess at his other job.

Sex, sex, sex, and more sex. Your old chap doesn't need a manual to teach him how to do it, he's happy to learn on the job, and with only one thing to think about and his own built-in radar he has a sure fire way of letting you know when opportunity knocks. He's always up for it, you won't hear him complaining, his mantra is "Sex, even when it ain't great it still pretty good" and, ever the optimist, he keeps his eye on the future and tells himself good times are coming.

OK, I'm there, sex is like oxygen, you only miss it when you ain't getting any.

Ooh yeah, sex, sex, sex and more sex. Light the candles, put the music on low and feel the temperature rise as the moment unfolds and the atmosphere throbs with anticipation. There's no need for words, she gives you that look that inflames your desire so you move closer and what the fuck, what's going on here? Looks like the old chap has gone on strike. A misfire in the trouser snake department, shit, never had one of those before, what a time to get a flat. What's a guy supposed to do now? Just extend the warm up in the hope it's just a temporary fault and pray that normal service will be resumed shortly, or cancel the event and suggest you check out what's on TV? And, if normal service is not resumed then the problem is gonna need fixing which means first it needs diagnosing and with that thought a thousand possible explanations begin to flash across your mind and so right now is probably a good time to check out the suck, squeeze, bang, blow of sex.

First thing to check is your nuts, still got two with no lumps or aches, no burning or claret in your pee and not constantly waking up in the night needing a leak so all looks good there. Best to check the back end while you're at it. Still dropping solid torpedoes on a regular basis so that all looks to be working too. That's a relief, and much as us guys don't look forward to it, if you have any suspicions, rather than take a risk with your life or your balls, you know the smart move is to go straight to the Doc because your health is priceless. Women rarely hesitate and love to tell us the Doc's seen it all before but what they don't understand is, that's not how it works in Man World. What they don't get is that we look inward for answers and we haven't put it all on display before so we need a moment to get comfortable with the idea and then we'll get straight down there. If you're happy that there is nothing physically wrong, and just to be doubly sure run your decision through your good and bad decision checker, the next thing to check is your lifestyle. Poor diet, too much of a good thing, not enough exercise, smoking, being overweight and too little sleep can all impact our bodies and leave us feeling a bit flat, and you can easily work out if you need to make any changes here. And while you're at it, read the leaflet to check the side effects of any pills or potions you may be taking because you never know what information you might find hidden in the small print.

As sure as night turns to day and day back to night sex will soon be back on the agenda for the simple reason that your other half has a libido too. So if you have ruled out health and lifestyle issues as the cause then we need to dig a little deeper to find out what is going on. And the good news is that our old buddies Mr G and Mr A have once again volunteered to share what they know with us and, just as with all problems, both guys say that having solved it they can now look back and laugh about it.

Mr A recalled a time his old chap appeared to have developed phallic amnesia and forgotten how to take care of business. His answer was to look back and notice what he had done differently in the last few days. Almost immediately an image of a doner kebab drenched in chilli sauce popped into his mind and this reminded him of the several beers that proceeded it and the stinging in his arse that followed it. And with that in mind Mr A instantly wrote the whole episode off as the result of too much beer and a dodgy kebab and, as per his expectation, his old chap was soon back to doing what he believes he was born to do.

Mr G, being a man accustomed to getting what he wants, found his experience to be rather more challenging. For him the picture was not so bright and the thought of sex felt more like a test than an invitation to a party, as Mr G put it, the thought of lovemaking made him stiffen up but sadly in all the wrong places. The thought of sex still got his attention, and he could easily recall the many happy times he had spent on the nest, but for now something was just not clicking the way it used to. Determined that he had definitely not had his last shag, Mr G knew that to solve his problem he needed to pinpoint the cause and from there he was confident he could use his tools and skills to create a solution that would soon have his old chap standing to attention again. And, so we can all fully understand how the problem worked and how to solve it, Mr G has laid it out from end to end for us, so if you ever find yourself here you will recognise where you are in the process and know exactly what to do next.

Casting his mind back Mr G replayed recent events so he could see exactly what was happening, just like he was watching himself in a movie. Using this technique allowed him to map the process with no emotional cost leaving him free to concentrate on the sequence of events. Although he still enjoyed the thought of sex, Mr G found that when his thoughts shifted to the idea of actually having sex his radar flashed up a danger signal and this alert caused his ECU to automatically load up it's "Avoid" programme. And this created a conflict in his mind, with one voice urging him to dive in and delight in great sex while the other suggested he pretend he had more urgent business elsewhere, because this ruse would allow him to avoid the situation and with it any potential negative outcome.

As he continued to watch his movie Mr G became aware that, up to now, he had taken the soft option and chosen to busy himself with anything rather than risk another let down and noticing this prompted Mr G to ask himself the magic question, why? Eu-fucking-reka, in an instant the dark clouds were replaced by a feeling of relief mixed with joy as the answer powered through to reveal itself. What he had been experiencing was performance anxiety, a state that will be easily recognised not just by guys who've had a flat but also by millions of guys who have had to give a public speech or maybe take a penalty in a shoot-out. Now he could see how things came to be what they were, the root cause was simply that his mind was not on the job, his suck, squeeze, bang, blow was not in tune with his objective, and so the result was not the one he wanted. And from here he could clearly see how the situation had evolved, he had taken a one-off event and generalised it into a one-size-fits-all rule and this had corrupted his sex programme on his ECU so when his thoughts turned to taking care of man business he automatically started to make dark pictures of things going wrong, overdubbed with a deadbeat soundtrack, and this, not surprisingly, left him feeling rather flat. And it was at this point Mr G realised that the anxiety he was feeling was all of his own making.

OK, I get it. It's true what they say, when it comes to sex if you ain't excited then nothing's gonna happen.

You ain't wrong there. And the key for Mr G was recalling that your conscious mind can only focus on one thing at a time, because this recollection led him to the realisation that the root of his problem was that he had been mis-directing his focus. Up to now, he had been making mental movies of things going wrong, which caused him to feel anxious when what he really wanted was the complete opposite. And it was at this point that Mr G recalled the good news, it's your mind and you have the power to decide what you want it to focus on. And from there he was able to give his suck, squeeze, bang, blow a tune-up to re-ignite his passion and get back on the nest. As Mr G puts it, "When you get it straight in your mind the rest just falls into place"

So now we all know that anxiety is just another feeling we learned to create inside ourselves and the great news is that you can learn to feel relaxed, confident and in control in all situations just as easily and coming up is a step-by-step guide of how to do exactly that.

But first here's some good news for guys who find the party is over quicker than they would like. In addition to the next exercise, because again the root of the problem can be a one-off event that has become generalised into a one-size-fits-all rule which has corrupted a guy's good sex programme, there are a number of other strategies you can use to put that challenge firmly in the past so you can get back to doing it the way you want to. One is to slow down time. As you rehearse in your mind slow everything down to half speed, so everything takes twice as long as before, because the root of the problem can be doing things on fast-forward, so slow down time in your mind and see what you'll see, hear what you'll hear and feel how good you'll feel. Or you could follow the advice Dom gave to Ted as he prepared for his big date with Mary in the film "There's Something About Mary" "Choke the chicken....

otherwise it's like you're walking around with a loaded gun" No further explanation required there but do remember that is part of the build-up and not the main event. And your fourth option is to look at it like a three course meal, the starter might have felt rushed but you can still take your time with the main course and dessert. You're best placed to work out which option will work best for you so feel free to check them all out.

Reversing Anxiety

1 Think about the thing that made you feel anxious.

2 Notice in which direction the feeling is moving in your body and give it a colour so that you can visualise it moving. It has to be moving, even if it feels like a knot, in order to keep triggering.

3 Vividly imagine taking the feeling out of your body so you can see it spinning in front of you. Spin it a little faster and notice how the feeling gets stronger and now slow it back to it's original speed.

4 Reverse the direction of the feeling and as you do change the colour to your favourite colour and pull the feeling back into your body so that you can feel it spinning in the opposite direction inside you.

5 Keep spinning the feeling in the opposite direction inside your body faster and faster as you notice yourself feeling differently as you spin out all of the old bad feeling.

6 Think of something that makes you feel really excited and motivated and notice the direction of the feeling.

7 Keep spinning this feeling as you vividly imagine doing the thing that used to bother you really well and see everything working out perfectly.

8 As you do this notice all the new possibilities that you can

see appearing in front of you now and begin your new life now.

OK, I can see how that one can work for any situation where a guy might have previously experienced a challenge and wants to feel sure he's got his A game back.

Yeah, it's certainly put a lot of guys back on top. I guess it proves that when you control your preparation you maximise your chances of getting the result you want.

And here's a late addition, Mrs G has been in touch, Mr G's in the loop so everything's cool, one of her buddies turned her on to this and she wanted to share it with the citizens of Man World and Girl World because it's a fix they can work together. Mrs G said she was all set to give it a run out, before Mr G sorted the issue for himself, adding that her buddy swears by it because now her other half can't leave her alone. So the story goes, if a guy is having a little trouser snake challenge this works wonders and the bonus is that it allows his other half to feel involved and that she has contributed to their triumph and here's how it works. They keep everything in their world the same except his Missus tells him the nest is off limits. He's going to cop an eye full every now and then, just through the normal course of events, but he's been told he's not allowed to touch. She didn't go into the detail of exactly how it works, she just said that this is one of those times when it's best to leave the mystery unsolved and that the most important thing was that it does work so what's not to like? And when the result is you end up with a massive boner and pleading with your Missus to let you park it she's probably right. As Mrs G said, what's not to like? If you're both happy to play and it gets the job done then it can only be a good thing.

Er, OK, Sounds like it could be fun and when it's working who cares how it works? And it's a much better idea than

them moaning at the poor fella, some girls just don't yet understand that complaining ain't gonna get you laid.

I'm with you on the first one and can see your point for the second one but I'm not sure I'd put it in those words.

14

It's The Dogs!

Here's a question for you, now you understand how the mechanics of anxiety work, and how to fix it, can you name the other situation where a one-off experience can lead to on-going challenges?

Er, no.

Here's a clue, in this instance, rather than building up bad pictures of what might happen to make themselves feel anxious, guys wait until the next time they are faced with the situation before switching on their hazard warning lights.

OK, I've got it, it's phobias.

Spot on. And the good news is that our buddy John has agreed to share his story with us so we can get a handle on the suck, squeeze, bang, blow of how phobias work. John says his challenge began one afternoon when he went out for a stroll to enjoy the sunshine. As he crossed the park that was a shortcut to his favourite beer garden he suddenly found his progress halted by an angry canine who displayed his bad humour by growling menacingly as he arched his back and bared his teeth. Finding himself rooted to the spot John's mind went into overdrive as he imagined what terrible mischief the dog may be planning. Was it just having a bad day, maybe it's just marking its territory or maybe it's an untamed throwback leaving them both at the mercy of its natural instincts. Whichever it was, John definitely wasn't comfortable with such thoughts and immediately, yet unconsciously, decided that all future encounters with such a creature would automatically trigger his internal alarm. And, with the dog deciding he had more urgent business elsewhere and his mental note safely filed away, he quickly forgot the incident as he turned his attention back to the now ever more welcome pint he was heading for.

Time passed by and, as John recalls, he never gave the the event a second thought. That was until the next time he encountered a specimen of mans best friend. Even though this one was on a lead and being led by its master, so logically it really did not represent a threat, John still found that his internal alarm sounded and his state changed from relaxed to high alert and he found himself once again rooted to the spot as thoughts of what devilish intent the dog may harbour rushed through his mind. As he calmed down, John began to question his reaction to his encounters with dogs and this led him to understand that he had unwittingly developed a phobic response and also to the conclusion that the smart move would be to find a way to separate the emotion from the event. John says that making the quality decision that he'd had enough and wanted to change was the basis for his being able to change because, not only did it prompt him to learn more about what he was dealing with, but he knew that when you back a desire with a strong will a positive outcome is inevitable.

And to help us fill in the gaps John has laid out what he discovered about phobias. Firstly, the building blocks of phobias are a one-off reference experience, either real or imagined, which then gets generalised into a one-size-fits-all rule. So a guy's first reaction to a one-off bad experience, be that a turbulent flight, getting stuck in a lift, buzzed by a wasp, menaced by a snarling dog or an encounter with a creepy-crawley becomes his automatic reaction every time he faces that set of circumstances. Secondly, he shows us how phobias differ from anxiety. Anxiety requires preparation, for a guy to feel anxious he has to first fill his head with dark thoughts whereas with phobias guys tend not to think about the event until the next time it occurs. And thirdly, John brings us some good news, because all phobias work the same way they can all can be swiftly and easily overcome and here is a step by step guide to walk you through how to do exactly that.

Fast Phobia Cure

1 Think of the phobia that you want to be free of.

2 Imagine yourself in a cinema and take a seat in the centre of the front row.

3 Float up out of your body and take a seat in the projector room so you can look down and see yourself sitting in the front row.

4 Put the beginning of the phobic event on the screen in the form of a coloured slide. From your seat in the projector room look down and see yourself sitting in the front row looking up at the screen and run the movie to the point where you again feel safe.

5 At the end of the movie freeze the frame into a slide. Change the picture to black and white and float down from the projector room back into the you who is sitting in the front row. Now step into yourself on the screen and run the movie backwards at tripple speed or faster so everything is happening in reverse. You can overlay some circus music if you choose to and when you get back to the beginning of the movie freeze-frame the image.

6 Walk back out of the still picture and sit back down in the centre of the front row and white out the whole screen.

7 Run through the steps 3-6 three or four more times or until you notice how you feel differently now when you think about the old phobia as you try in vain to recall the old feelings.

OK, I get it, anxiety and phobias are both fears that we create inside ourselves and the key to beating both is to unleash the power of the ECU between my ears.

Correct, got it in one. And the truth is neither John nor you were ever fearful of the event, you were fearful of your thoughts about the event and the good news is that you already have all the tools you need to take full control of your thoughts so now you can quickly overcome any challenge you encounter and guarantee yourself a smooth and speedy passage to your Promised Land.

15

Road Clear Ahead

We've covered a lot of ground together and now we're on the home straight. Now you know how your suck, squeeze, bang, blow, your think, feel, act process works and you've built yourself a toolbox of techniques so you find it easy to keep yourself in-tune and maintain your focus. You know what living the dream in your Promised Land means for you and you've got an action plan for how you're gonna get there and a firm timescale for when you'll arrive. From your fellow citizens you've learned about the challenges that try to creep up on us here in Man World and a host of positive strategies to innoculate yourself against them so everytime you think of your future you see a big, bright and bold picture so your commitment never wavers.

OK, I'm with you there and another thing I've definitely learned is that there is no reason to hesitate I just do everything as best I can and trust that perfection will come with practice.

You're right there, because taking positive action builds both momentum and belief and with your ever growing belief who knows what amazing feats you'll choose to accomplish in the future? You've already learned how to fire up your internal simulator to gain insight and maximise your talents so this time we're going one step further, this time we're going to learn how you can learn the skills of how to do it from the elite performers in any field of endeavour you choose. And so, with that in mind, let's take a look at how some of our fellow citizens of Man World calibrated their suck, squeeze, bang, blow as they prepared to dazzle us with their brilliance. And your first job here is to think of a situation that you feel would really test a guy.

Er, taking a penalty in a shoot-out to win the the World Cup Final.

Good one, and that's exactly the situation our buddy Fabio Grosso found himself in when Italy played France in the 2006 final. So what was Fabio really faced with? Could securing victory really be as simple as taking a shot at goal from 12 yards with only the keeper to beat, especially as the keeper is not allowed to move until the ball is struck? Or were there other factors to consider? Factors such as half of the spectators in the stadium hoping he'd miss, 61 million of his fellow Italian's back home praying he'd score, a TV audience running into the billions and the greatest prize in world football at stake. Add in those details and it's easy to see both how a guy could feel tested and the benefit of being able to control your focus and emotions.

And the good news for Fabio and his 61 million teammates is that he scored and the good news for all the rest of us guys is that he shared with us exactly how he tuned his suck, squeeze, bang, blow as he prepared to take the kick.

"The wait was long, that walk too. Maybe the whole of my career passed through my mind during that short journey. I didn't hear much around me, maybe the concentration was so intense that around me there was almost a vacuum. Then what happened happened"

Take a moment now to re-read Fabio's story and as you do step into his boots, feel yourself there in the moment now and experience the event for yourself and as you do notice how you suddenly feel super confident that you too would be successful in those circumstances.

OK, done that and I see what you mean, the way I feel now I'd deffo have money on myself to score. And it's a great way to practice and polish my new skills too.

I'd go along with that, and here's another example for you to check out. This one is from another big game, the Championship Play-Off Final. To set the scene for you it's May 31st 1999 and Watford are playing Bolton at Wembley stadium watched by a crowd of 70,000. At stake for each Club is a place in the Premier League and £80 million of revenue, at stake for the players is the chance to live their dream of playing in what is regarded to be the best league in the world and at stake for the fans is the chance to watch their team achieve glory and share in the adventure that would follow. And again, when you add in those details it's easy to see how the guys from both teams could feel tested and the benefit of being able to control your focus and emotions.

38 minutes into the game Watford win a corner, the ball is crossed into the area, a defender makes a headed clearance and, as Fabio would say, then what happened happened.

And what happened is that Nick Wright scored one of the greatest goals ever seen on the planet with a perfectly executed overhead kick, a goal that not only put his team on course for victory but also wrote his name into the record books and made him a Watford FC legend. And again, the good news for the rest of us guys is that he shared with the Watford FC website exactly how he tuned his suck, squeeze, bang, blow as he readied himself to do what he did.

"It was something very instinctive. I did weigh up the situation, there wasn't really an easy pass on. I think if there was an easy pass on chances are I would've taken it. I would've laid it back to somebody. But there wasn't, so it's about taking the chance, trusting the training you've done, the hours of practice, making sure you time the impact and contact of the ball really well."

Now take a moment to re-read Nick's story and as you do step into his boots, feel yourself there in the moment now and experience the event for yourself and as you do notice how once again you suddenly feel super confident that you too would have scored.

OK, done that and it definitely works. When I stepped into their boots and did it their way it felt like success was guaranteed and the voice in my head was shouting "Focus, you can nail this"

And the reason for that is because you were sharing Fabio and Nick's mind set, their suck, squeeze, bang, blow, a mind set that made the task appear easy. A mind set that in Fabio's case allowed him to put himself in a vacuum so his focus was solely on his objective and in Nick's case one that allowed him to be fully in the moment so he was able weigh up his options and select the best one in just a few short seconds. And for both guys it was their mind set that allowed them to display their technical skill by perfectly executing a physical task in the heat of battle. And the good news is the next exercise will allow you to step into the boots of anyone you choose and learn from them just as you did with Fabio and Nick. The idea behind the exercise is that you become that person for a short time and then, having collected the insights you want, you step back out of them and back into yourself bringing all you have learned with you. To get the best from this exercise it helps to know a little about the background and career of your subject, because that will allow you to not just stand in their boots but to really get inside their skin. So when you have selected the guys you want to learn from take a moment to do some research on them if you feel it's needed. You can check them out on Wikipedia, watch their videos on YouTube or read their autobiography or any other books they have written.

Deep Trance Identification Exercise

1 Relax and make a life size 3D image of the person you want to learn from standing in front of you.

2 Remind yourself that you are only going to become that person for a short period of time and that when you have collected the information you want you will return to being your normal self bringing only the learnings back with you.

3 Step into your subject and stand with their posture, speak with their voice tone, match their breathing and thoughts so you feel like you are becoming them and can see and experience the world as they do.

4 As you tune in to being them focus on what objective you want to achieve and ask yourself these questions. What should I do more of? What should I do less of? What should I do next? What should I avoid?

5 Take a moment to consider the answers and accept only those you feel have positive value.

6 Say thanks to your subject for their help and step back out of them and back into your normal self bringing all you have learned with you.

7 Update your action plan and begin immediately to put your new knowledge to work for you.

OK, I'm in. I'm on a hat-trick here so I know the technique works and when I add it to all the others I've learned I can see that a whole new world of possibilities has opened up for me.

Good stuff, I guess whoever said it first was right, success is a journey and not a destination. And now you know that when you take charge of your think, feel, act process the world really is your oyster. And with that in mind always remember all you have learned and always practice all you have learned and as you fire off your anchor stack now enjoy feeling good, feeling confident, feeling successful, feeling motivated and feeling lucky because now you know the road is clear ahead.

Printed in Great Britain
by Amazon.co.uk, Ltd.,
Marston Gate.